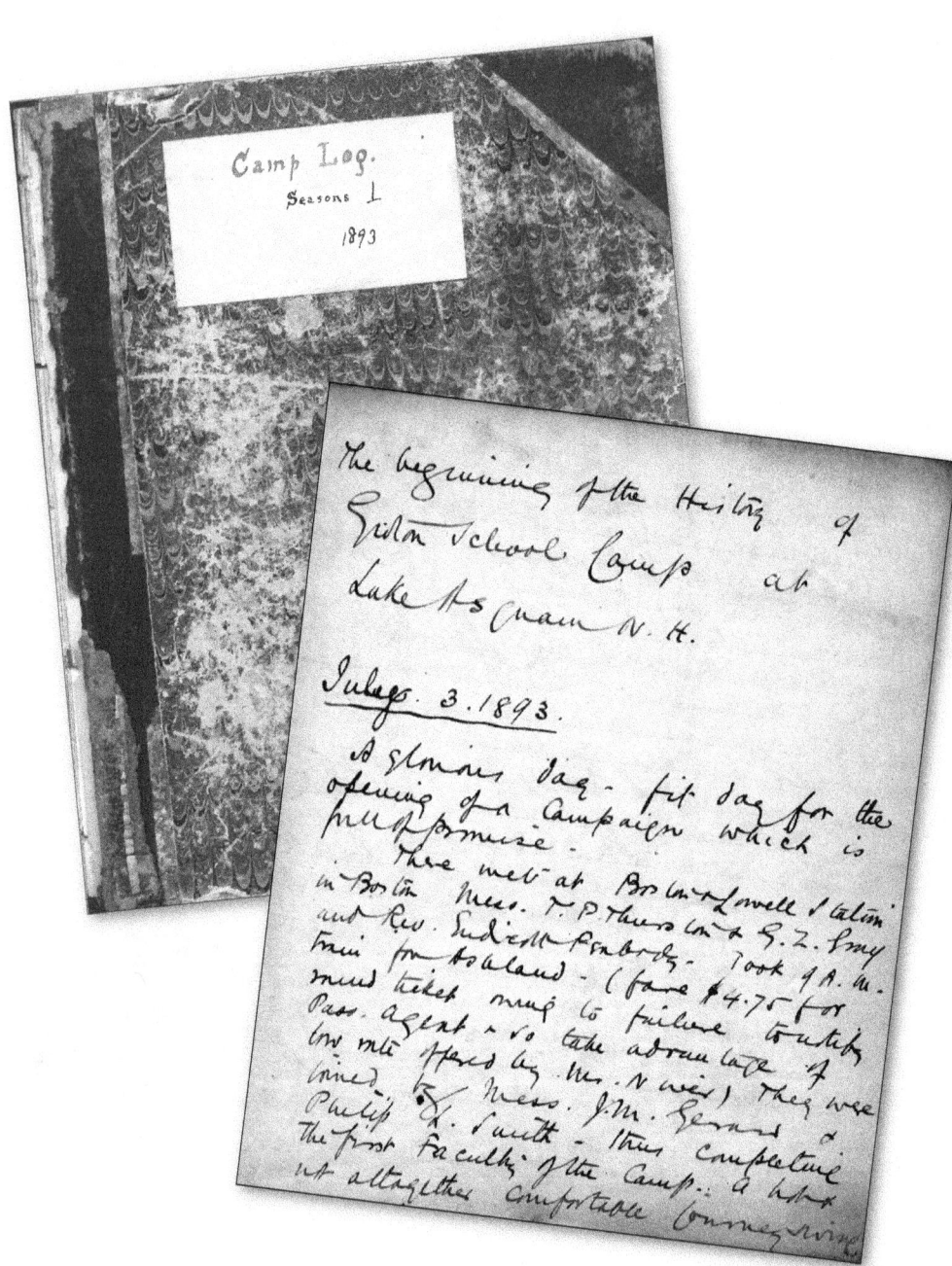

Original 1893 Camp Journal (see complete journal beginning on page 99

Courtesy of Bill Hemmel, Lakes Region Aerial

The Chapel—Groton School   *Groton Massachusetts*

–Franklin Delano Roosevelt–
Esteemed Groton School Alum

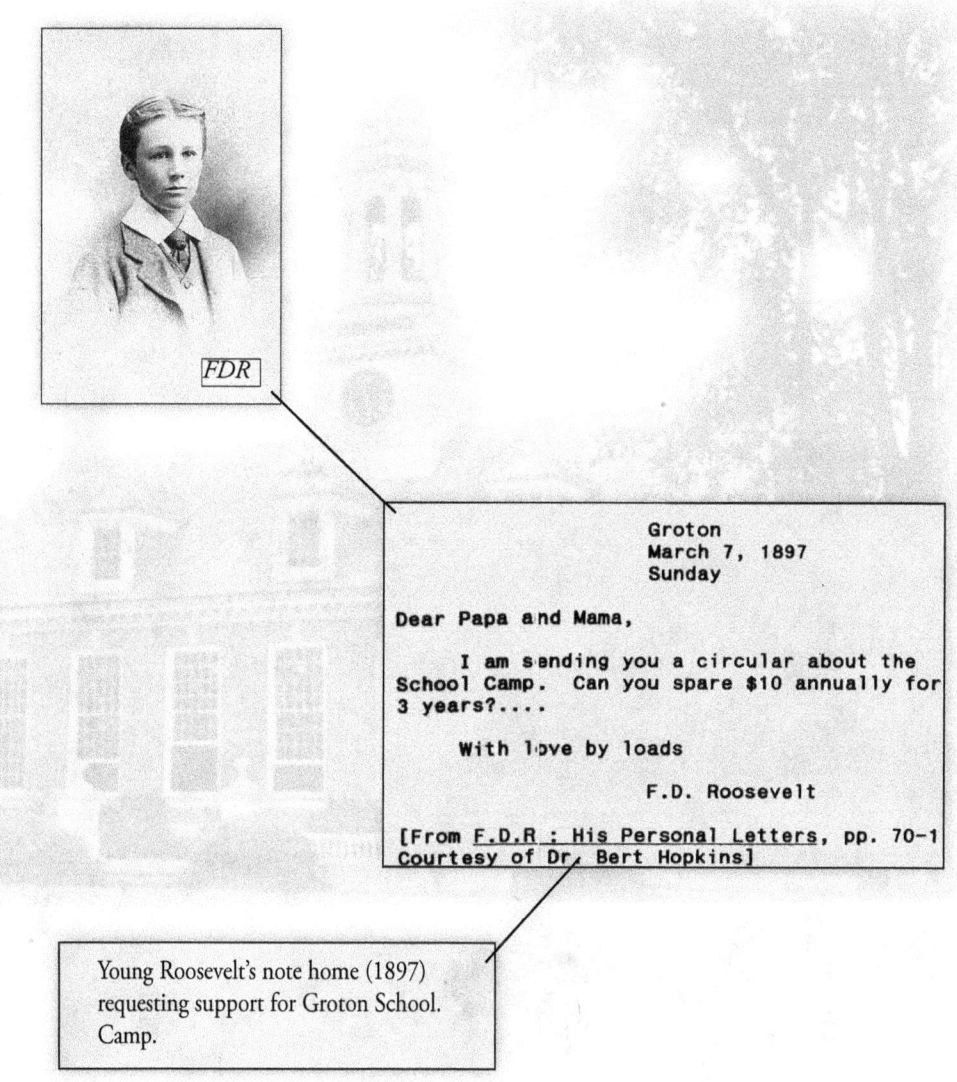

```
                              Groton
                              March 7, 1897
                              Sunday

Dear Papa and Mama,

    I am sending you a circular about the
School Camp.  Can you spare $10 annually for
3 years?....

        With love by loads

                              F.D. Roosevelt

[From F.D.R : His Personal Letters, pp. 70-1
Courtesy of Dr. Bert Hopkins]
```

Young Roosevelt's note home (1897) requesting support for Groton School Camp.

Ever mindful of the welfare of our youth, President Franklin Roosevelt signs the "Fair Labor Standards Act" into law in 1938. It prohibits the employment of children under the age of 16.

GROTON SCHOOL CAMP

1893

SQUAM LAKE, N.H.

A History Of The First Summer Camp For
Underprivileged Boys
(The Progressive Era)

—Now Named The Mayhew Program—
A Year-round Preventative Program
For "At-risk" Boys

By
Kenneth E. Bingham

BINGHAMUS PRESS
Jorden2323@msn.com

Copyright © 2009 by Trustees of The Mayhew Program
All rights reserved
First Edition

Library of Congress Control Number: 2009901518

Bingham, Kenneth E.
   Groton School Camp : 1893, Squam Lake, N.H. : a history of the first summer camp for underprivileged boys (the Progressive Era) / by Kenneth E. Bingham. -- 1st ed.

   p. : ill. ; cm.

   Includes index.
   "Now named the Mayhew Program - a year-round preventative program for 'at-risk' boys."
   ISBN: 978-0-578-00841-7

1. Groton School Camp (N.H.)--History. 2. Camps--New Hampshire--Squam Lakes--History. 3. Social work with children--New Hampshire--20th century. I. Title.

GV194 . N4 G76 2009
796.54/09742   2009901518

Childhood And Child Welfare In The Progressive Era By James Marten. Copyright © 2005. Used With Permission By Bedford/st. Martin's Publishers.

History Of Organized Camping By Eleanor Eells. Reprinted With Permission By The American Camping Association, Inc. Copyright © 1986.

1893 Groton School Camp Journal. Pictures, And The 1901 And 1942 Grotonian Used With Permission By The Groton School Of Groton Massachusetts.

The Mayhew Program, Used With Permission

Compilation, Cover, And Book Design By Kenneth E. Bingham

Front Cover; Outline Of Red Hill, Squam Lake NH

Acknowledgments

SPECIAL THANKS TO DOUG BROWN—Groton School faculty member—and the wonderful Groton School of Groton, Massachusetts for their hospitality and friendly assistance in the gathering of the G.S. Camp archives. Thanks also to Bill Polk, Jack Richards, Dave Howe, John Tyler, Bill Hoyt, Jon Choate, Pat Bingham, Joe Bingham, Jerry Williamson, Sam Chauncey, Doug Dyke, Dave Lincoln, Ken Chisholm, Jim Nute, Bruce Gladstone, Charles Johnson, Patricia Fry, Jim Hodson, Dave Ruell (Ashland Historical Society), Roger Larachelle, Bill Hempel, Bruce Collins, Timothy Buckley and Richard Bingham.

*To Reverend Endicott Peabody—who practiced what he preached
—and made it happen*

William Armory Gardner, Endicott Peabody, and Sherrard Billings—1884

FOREWORD
By Bill Polk

Bill Polk graduated from Groton School in 1958, He attended Trinity College, and Union Theological Seminary, He taught at Athens College, and the Lawrenceville School, before becoming the headmaster of Groton School, a position he held for twenty-five years. He served as a counselor at the Groton School Camp in 1957, 1959, and 1960. Now retired, Bill lives in Cambridge, Ma.

I FIRST SAW MAYHEW ISLAND IN JUNE 1956, as part of a group, counselors and kitchen crew, who arrived on the island to open up the camp. We corked the boats, put the dock in the water, dug holes for the "mines"[1], swept the floors, and pumped water through the old fire extinguishers to chase the bats out of the main building.

Two of us were assigned to go to Boston to accompany the campers back to New Hampshire, never a choice assignment. The train arrived in Ashland, the yellow school buses took us to the lake, and with veteran campers rowing and the new campers quivering, we set out for the island in the newly but imperfectly corked boats. The day was unusually windy and the water unusually choppy. Approaching the island, we saw the dock come loose and start floating rapidly down the lake. Whoever was in the outboard sped off to retrieve the dock while six, or was it eight, boats maneuvered around the island to land on the beach. Thus started what would be for me three wonderful summers at the Groton School Camp.

Near the end of the my first summer's final session, some of us counselors gathered on the back deck of the Fac Shack to carve our initials in the deck, each trying to get ours as close as possible to FDR's. As the future president did, so did we want to leave our mark on the camp. Down deep we knew that the camp left a much larger mark on us.

---

[1] *Mines are outhouses.*

That becomes abundantly clear in the following pages. As a labor of love, from his home in California and his assignment in Iraq, Ken Bingham has edited the history of the Groton School Camp. The remembrances along with the pictures bring to life for the reader many memories that confirm not only the fun we experienced at the Camp, but also the valuable life lessons that left a mark on us.

> Bill Polk
> Camp Counselor – 1957, 1959, 1960
> Softball Team – Polk's Toasties
> Cambridge, Ma
> December 2007

—The years will tell—what the days never know—

Contents

ACKNOWLEDGMENTS: xi

FOREWORD: xiii

INTRODUCTION: xvii

PART I: THE PROGRESSIVE ERA: *The Changing View Of The Child*
        Chapter 1   Childhood And Child Welfare In The Progressive Era   3

PART II: HISTORY OF ORGANIZED CAMPING: *First 100 Years*
        Chapter 2   History of Organized Camping 33

Part III: GROTON SCHOOL CAMP HISTORY
        Chapter 3   Groton Scholars Start a Camp 41
        Chapter 4   Groton School Camp History, (1) 1901 59
        Chapter 5   Groton School Camp History, (2) 1942 69
        Chapter 6   GSC History; Articles, Letters & Records 75

Part IV: THE 1893 GROTON SCHOOL CAMP JOURNAL
        Chapter 7   Groton School Camp Journal, 1893—— July 3 97
        Chapter 8   Groton School Camp Journal, 1893—— July 17 129
        Chapter 9   Groton School Camp Journal, 1893—— July 26 141
        Chapter 10   Groton School Camp Journal, 1893—— Aug. 6 153
        Chapter 11   Groton School Camp Journal, 1893—— Aug. 16 167
        Chapter 12   Groton School Camp Journal, 1893—— Aug. 27 185

Part V: THE NEWFOUND LAKE ERA 1920-1966
        Chapter 13   G.S.C., Mayhew Isle., Newfound Lake 1920-1966 201

Part VI: THE CURRENT PROGRAM, THE MAYHEW PROGRAM
        Chapter 14;   The Mayhew Program 259

Groton School, Groton Massachusetts
Founder of the Groton School Camp

F OUNDED in 1884 by Reverend Endicott Peabody. Groton's original aims included the intellectual, moral and physical development of its students in grades seven through twelve toward preparation for both college and "the active work of life". Now a coeducational, primarily residential school of 175 girls and 175 boys in grades eight through twelve, we set for our students the highest standards of academic achievement, intellectual growth, ethical awareness and behavior, sportsmanship, athletic endeavor and service to others.

The School takes leadership seriously, and our concern for character is a point of distinction. Our mission has never been narrowly to prepare students for college, but rather always to provide an experience which, while academically rigorous, goes far beyond college requirements, addressing important personal aspects of growth and maturity. Through the years the means of achieving our aims have changed, yet Groton's size and its particular balance of tradition and innovation continue to provide exceptional opportunities to deserving students from diverse social, geographic, ethnic, and socio-economic backgrounds. Our unflagging commitment to each student's intellectual, moral, and physical growth and to the considerable resources of faculty, facility, and locale creates a school which is larger than the sum of its parts.

Groton believes in the notion that teachers should take part in students lives. Groton's faculty does what the best faculties do: it supports the highest level of academic activity, but it also creates a special form of life for the student. This relationship between students and faculty reaches beyond the classroom and affirms and nurtures the spirit as it challenges the mind. In this way, the faculty fulfill the founding vision that Groton teachers take up the teaching profession as their lifes work.

From the Grotn School web site—http://www.groton.org/home/home.asp

Introduction

ONE HUNDRED AND FIFTEEN YEARS AGO, Groton School's Missionary Society of Groton, Massachusetts, decided to start a summer camp for "underprivileged" boys of the Boston area. They established the Camp on Willoughby's Island[1] along the banks of Asquam Lake in New Hampshire, and they welcomed the first group of boys on July 5, 1893. The first of its type in the nation, Groton School Camp was more than just a place for boys to experience the out-of-doors. It represented a new social movement which the Reverend Endicott Peabody[2]—headmaster of Groton School—and his brethren—helped pioneer.

PART ONE OF THIS BOOK IS FROM JAMES MARTEN'S *CHILDHOOD AND CHILD WELFARE IN THE PROGRESSIVE ERA* (Bedford/St. Martin's Publishers, Copyright © 2005). In his book, Marten documents the problems of America's children during the turn of the nineteenth century, resulting primarily from industrialization, immigration and over-crowded cities. Marten's documentation helps explain why camps like Groton School Camp and many other child welfare programs—which were the hallmark of the "Progressive Era" (roughly 1890-1920)—came into being. This era—with it's growing middle class— ushered in a change in our culture's perception of the child and what childhood could and should be.

James Marten sums up the psychological changes toward American youth during this era with the following passage:

> —*Rather than measuring the value of children by the work they could do or the income they could produce—traditional measures of the "worth" of children, especially in agricultural societies—the urban middle class drew value from the emotional relationships parents formed with their children.*[3]—

---

[1] *Now named Groton Island, and Squam Lake. Squam Lake was also the setting of the famous movie "On Golden Pond".*

[2] *The Reverend Endicott Peabody also established the famous Groton School, in Groton, Mass. in 1884 (see page opposite). He established the first Episcopal Church in Arizona-(Tombstone 1882)- during the rough and tumble days that included the Earp brothers, Geronimo and the infamous "Boot Hill".*

[3] *From James Marten's book, Childhood and Child Welfare in the Progressive Era.*

IN PART TWO, THE AUTHOR DRAWS FROM ELEANOR ELLS' BOOK, *HISTORY OF ORGANIZED CAMPING* (American Camping Association, Inc. Copyright © 1986), which provides additional commentary and perspective regarding this unique American social movement.

PART THREE PRESENTS THE CAMP HISTORY ON SQUAM which includes articles from the 1901 and 1942 Groton School Quarterly (*Grotonian*), as told in the Camp founder's own words. In addition, the author has reproduced the 1893 camp journal which chronicles the daily adventures of the boys and the leaders of the Camp on Squam Lake. Camp photos and related peripheral history are included to give an idea and sense of the times.

PART FOUR DESCRIBES THE CAMP YEARS ON NEWFOUND LAKE BETWEEN 1920-1966.

PART FIVE FEATURES THE PRESENT DAY PROGRAM—"The Mayhew Program." Not only is this wonderful organization keeping the Groton School Camp traditions alive, but it provides a summer camping experience for "at-risk" boys, and oversees the boys' progress on a year-round basis.

This book is an ode to the Groton School Camp and the Mayhew Program, and serves as a historical memorial to the people who took the important step from being socially aware, to the more important step of actively serving.

Michael D. Eisner, former Disney CEO—a camper and leader himself at Camp Keewaydin Vermont—recently wrote the book *CAMP*. His final words in the book read:

> —*Today, no matter how daunting the task in front of me, I think of that canoe, that trip, that experience, that early education. I believe Pepe and Q will do the same. Today, no matter what's in front of me, I think of Waboos and I think of camp.*[1]—

Kenneth E. Bingham
Nov. 2008

---

[1] *From Michael D. Eisner, book "Camp"; (Former CEO of The Walt Disney Company) Copyright © by the Eisner Foundation, Inc.*

Photo by Lewis Hine

Part I

The Progressive Era
1890's-1920's

A Changing View Of The Child

—Rather than measuring the value of children by the work they could do or the income they could produce—traditional measures of the "worth" of children, especially in agricultural societies—the urban middle class drew value from the emotional relationships parents formed with their children.— James Marten

Picture from James Marten's book, "Childhood and Child Welfare in the Progressive Era."

Chapter 1
Childhood and Child Welfare in the Progressive Era
by James Marten

This section[1]—by Dr. James Marten— is included to explain the social factors that led up to the need for camps like Groton School Camp, and other child welfare programs.

James Marten received his Ph.D. from University of Texas at Austin in 1986 and is currently professor of history at Marquette University in Milwaukee, where he teaches courses on the Civil War and on children's history. He is the author of The Children's Civil War (1998), which was selected as an Outstanding Academic Book by Choice Magazine and chosen for the Jesuit National Book Award in 1999. He is also the editor of Children and War: A Historical Anthology (2002). He serves as director of the Children in Urban America Project, an NEH-funded on-line archive of documents related to the history of children in Milwaukee. Marten is a founding member and secretary-treasurer of the Society for the History of Children and Youth. In 1999 he was a Fulbright Lecturer at Northeast Normal University in Changchun, People's Republic of China.

THE PROGRESSIVE ERA—roughly 1890 to 1920—remains a unique historical period, the first of several periods of reform and innovation in the twentieth century. In 1911, Susan Glaspell, a Chicago journalist and playwright, came up with the elegant phrase—"Science placing her gifts in the outstretched hands of Democracy"—thus capturing perfectly the ways that early-twentieth-century reformers hoped they could improve the lives of American children. Many of the ideas put forward during this time had been brewing for years and would continue to influence reformers and policy makers for decades.

Progressivism attracted men and women of all political persuasions; both the Democrat Woodrow Wilson and the Republican Theodore Roosevelt considered themselves Progressives. Uniting all Progressives was what Roosevelt called a "fierce discontent of evil"—of those people and forces that worked against fairness, justice, and equality in the United States. To combat this evil, Progressives placed their confidence in scientific research—one must find out what is wrong before one can change it—and in the capacity of professionally trained experts to manage and reform social problems. Another common Progressive belief was that local, state, and federal governments must take the lead in establishing a fair economy, raising the standard

[1] *Used with permission. Copyright © 2005 by Bedford/St. Martin. Pictures added by editor 2008*

of living for everyone, and bringing the nation's vast resources to bear on the many problems facing Americans, especially in crowded cities.

Progressive reforms at the national level included regulating trusts, lowering tariffs on imports, achieving women's suffrage, prohibiting alcohol, regulating the packaging of food and the sale of drugs, and preserving the environment. At the state level, Progressives established processes for holding referendums to consider legislation, recalling elected officials, and regulating child labor. At the local level, reformers in many cities reduced the size of city councils, hired city managers to break the power of corrupt political bosses, and made public utilities out of urban transportation, power, and sewer systems.

There were many causes and inspirations for this coming together of diverse political parties and interest groups. Some reformers were concerned by the soaring number of foreigners flooding American cities, others by the expanding gulf between the rich and poor, still others by the disorder caused by political corruption and labor strife. Although Progressives did not completely ignore rural America, they were far more interested in the chaotic cities bursting with immigrants and social problems. Many acted out of compassion for the less fortunate, while others feared that without a coherent approach to poverty, crime, political corruption, and urban hygiene, to name only a few targets of change, society was in danger of falling apart. The only solution was to impose discipline and fairness on society. Progressives were engaged, in the famous words of the historian Robert H. Wiebe, in a "search for order," and the programs they designed to confront the problems of the cities reflected that imperative.

Similar motivations led to conflicting results. For instance, whereas northern political reformers aimed to "clean up" politics by eliminating city bosses, southern Progressives sought to "clean up" the violence and corruption in their states by disfranchising the African Americans against whom most of that violence and corruption was directed.

Child welfare became the issue that most Progressives could agree on. The most popular reforms among Progressive activists were related to children: juvenile justice, playgrounds, pensions for widowed mothers, health care and housing. Child labor laws received almost unanimous support from the various branches of the Progressive movement. As innocent victims and as the hope for America's future, children had to be protected. They represented all that was good about the country, and the way they were treated reflected the nation's values and priorities.

Another characteristic of Progressive thought that deeply affected child welfare efforts was nostalgia for the small towns in which many reformers had grown up. The Boston social worker Philip Davis, in his widely read *Street-Land: Its Little People and Big Problems,* revealed a powerful longing for the values and conditions of small towns in arguing that the "sights and sounds" of the city are foreign to ideal childhood. Beauty is everywhere suppressed. "Birds" and "flowers" are mere spelling words to many city children. Dull and loud colors blur each other. Wild noises fill the air. Americans' affection for traditional small towns—like the little Illinois town in which Jane Addams lived as a girl—would spur Progressives to create programs characterized by interpersonal contact, wholesome entertainment and leisure activities, and a sometimes naïve sense of fair play.

A final element of the Progressive mind-set was the Social Gospel movement that emerged in the United States in the 1880s. Led by Protestant clergy and lay activists and advocated by many Roman Catholic priests and Jewish rabbis, the Social Gospel grew from the recognition that not all Americans benefited equally from the American economic and political systems. The sometimes bloody labor unrest that occured in the country from the 1870s through the 1890s reflected deep divisions in American society; unlike the businessmen who crushed labor unions and the politicians who sent troops to put down strikes, reformers believed that understanding and compassion for the working and immigrant classes would be much more effective than force. Progressives like Theodore Roosevelt and Jane Addams were guided at least in part by their religious faith, which inspired them to use public and private resources to bring fairness and hope into the lives of the underprivileged and foreign-born.

These assumptions led reformers to construct fairly narrow paths through which all children were supposed to pass. They often ignored ethnic, religious, and economic differences in their efforts to ensure that all children shared the same opportunities and enjoyed the same advantages. But they did not ignore race. African Americans were encouraged to participate in Progressive reforms, but they did so in segregated facilities and organizations. And despite the fact that most reformers were not working on behalf of a particular religious denomination, moral indignation influenced their perceptions and ideals. The goals of the new generation of reformers might not include conversion, but they certainly included a well-developed sense of right and wrong and a moral imperative that would have been familiar to earlier, denomination-based reformers. Indeed, the facts uncovered by reformers' surveys, seemingly objective interview techniques, and compilation of statistics were often accompanied by sentimental and judgmental language condemning corporations, ignorant and abusive parents (mostly immigrants), and uncaring and corrupt local governments.

TOWARD AN IDEAL CHILDHOOD
Observers had not always been so sympathetic to the poor and needy children in American cities. In 1849, New York City's chief of police, George W. Matsell, reported on the "increasing number of vagrants, idle and vicious children of both sexes, who infest our public thoroughfares, hotels, docks" and "are growing up in ignorance and profligacy." These youngsters, he predicted, were "destined to a life of misery, shame and crime, and ultimately to a felon's doom." The chief blamed their "always careless, generally intemperate and oftentimes immoral and dishonest parents" for the plight of the children, but nevertheless complained that the youngsters, who were "addicted to immoralities of the most loathsome description," had become a "festering fountain," creating "a ceaseless stream to our lowest brothels, to the penitentiary and the state's prison."

Two generations later the Swedish sociologist Ellen Key declared that the twentieth century

Mullen's Alley by Jacob Riis, 1885

would be the "Century of the Child," an era of understanding and compassion. She promoted educational processes that depended less on rote learning and more on the ways that children actually learned; encouraged parents, especially mothers, to take a more active interest in their children; and argued that better parenting and schooling would not only lead to better lives for children, but would also solve long-standing social problems and create a better world. American reformers embraced Key's optimism and ideas and frequently borrowed the phrase, which reflected their high hopes and serious purposes.

The vast differences in the attitudes expressed by Matsell and Key reflect the shift in ideas about children that had been developing for decades before the Progressive Era. Although only a minority of American children could enjoy it, the optimistic, nurturing, and child-centered ideal became a powerful model to which many Americans aspired. More important, the assumptions it contained were applied to the problems facing city children by most urban reformers, at least some of whom believed that there was an "ideal" childhood and that society should enable all children to live that ideal.

The rise of this "child-nurture" philosophy of child-rearing was directly linked to the growth of the urban middle class, which dominated the reform movements of the Progressive Era. Then, as now, the term *middle class* was somewhat hard to define. Ranking below the "upper 10 percent," as the wealthy were often called, but above the struggling working classes, the middle class comprised small businesspeople and bureaucrats, independent farmers and urban professionals, white-collar workers and teachers, clerks and small manufacturers. A recent history of Progressivism argues that these diverse groups united in their concern over the deterioration of the social fabric in the United States, which they blamed on the indifference of the upper class and the poverty of the lower class. The middle class criticized the wealthiest Americans for their excesses. The working poor, however debased their lifestyles, were largely seen to be the victims of ignorance and powerlessness. Both groups needed to be reformed, and although middleclass Progressives did promote reforms directed at the wealthy—they spent most of their time on repairing the lives of the poor.

Midde-class reformers thought about childhood in the context of their own lives and attitudes. And although they did focus some of their energy on children from their own class—on public schools, especially—they also projected their images of the ideal childhood onto the working class. However, the comfort, safety, and security that the expanding middle class was able to provide for its children and that had come to be associated with a "normal" childhood were almost impossible to achieve for working-class families, especially in American cities. In other words, many Progressive child welfare programs were inspired by living standards that the middle class had come to expect and that working-class and most immigrant families could hardly dream of.

For instance, the number of children born to American families decreased markedly during the century after 1820. In 1830, there were 128 people under the age of twenty for every 100 people twenty and over (among whites). By 1890, the number had plunged to seventy-nine;

Photos by Jacob Riis

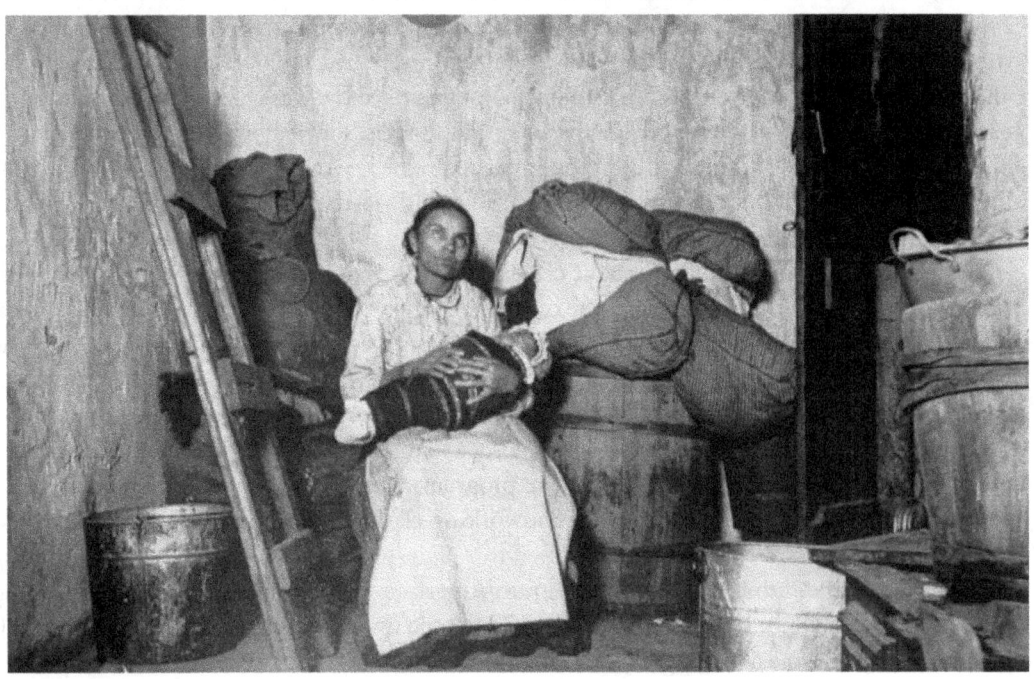

in 1920 it was only sixty-six. In urban areas only fifty-six young people for every 100 adults in 1920. Many immigrant families and working-class families continued to have large numbers of children, and the percentage of young people under the age of twenty living in American cities remained as high as 45 percent.

These statistics are important because reformers typically commented on the large number of children in the neediest families. And they could not help but compare the desperation of those families' lives to their own comfortable existence. By the turn of the twentieth century the steady decline in family size had already produced significant changes in child-rearing practices and in the material lives of children. They were *given* more room—literally and figuratively—and enjoyed greater privacy and opportunities to develop their own interests. Beginning in the mid-nineteenth century, the commercial publishing and toy industries began to take over the play and leisure time of children. Nurseries and children's bedrooms were filled with mass-produced toys and books and magazines published exclusively for children. From lurid dime novels and the titillating fare of nickelodeons to the slightly more respectable and uplifting stories of Horatio Alger and ever-popular magazines like *Youth's Companion,* children, especially in cities and towns, had more entertainment options than ever before. One poll in 1911 discovered that on any given day in New York City, one out of eight children attended a movie. Even more spectacular were the number of amusement parks opening around the country at the turn of the century. Coney Island, for example, drew a million people—many of them youngsters and teenagers—every summer. Conversely, although poor children were also eager consumers of movies and other cheap entertainment, they and their families enjoyed few other urban comforts. As middle-class families moved into roomy townhouses or bungalows in the suburbs, the poor in American cities were lucky to get a tiny apartment, where six, eight, or perhaps a dozen family members crowded into two rooms—and sometimes took in boarders. More than 80,000 tenements housed millions of New York City dwellers by 1900. These five or six-story, poorly constructed buildings were divided into tiny apartments with no indoor plumbing. Rows of dilapidated outdoor toilets were crowded in back of the buildings with severely inadequate ventilation. The Jewish section on the Lower East Side contained half a million people per single mile, one of the highest population densities in history. New York's housing situation was more extreme than that in most cities, but all the fast-growing urban areas in the industrial North were plagued by deteriorating neighborhoods, where largely immigrant populations were crammed into substandard housing. Another set of opposing factors helps explain both Progressivism and the problems that Progressives sought to eradicate. Combined with a general rise in income, especially among the urban middle class, smaller family size made it easier to stretch material and emotional resources, raising the standard of living for many children and enabling more Americans to nurture their children properly. Fewer children had to work outside the home; more could go to school for longer periods of time; and more could benefit from the social and cultural opportunities that abounded in the city. Rather than measuring the value of children by the work they could do or the income they could produce—traditional measures of the "worth" of children, especially in agricultural societies— the urban middle class drew value the emotional relationships parents formed with their children. This emotional investment in children was reflected in the increasing importance placed on expensive funerals for deceased children and other symbolic manifestations of affection and devotion. At the community level, it was reflected in the public outrage over the deaths of children in automobile and streetcar accidents during the first two decades of the twentieth century."

Although working-class parents also cherished their children, they simply could not afford to keep them out of the workforce. Between 1870 (the first year in which the U.S. Census recorded child labor) and 1900, the percentage of children between the ages of ten and fourteen who worked for wages increased from 16 percent to 22 percent (it may have been higher), and those figures did not account for the tens of thousands who labored in the "street trades" or as tenement-bound "home workers." Advocates for stricter child labor laws highlighted the injuries and long-term health problems caused by working in coal mines, cotton mills, and foundries, as well as the lack of educational and cultural opportunities available to child workers. Of course, the statistics were more complicated than reformers let on: They did not include the large percentage of child laborers who worked on farms. This was another case of middle-class Americans' belief in the benefits of rural living and outdoor work, which were thought to be inherently more healthy and more likely to build character than urban and factory labor. But the percentage of working children who lived in cities rose dramatically between 1870 and 1920, from 47 percent to nearly 75 percent. An early-twentieth-century study of several cities discovered 17,669 children selling newspapers; the Department of Commerce estimated in 1916 that "junkers"— mostly children—collected $265 million worth of scrap metal and ten million pounds of wastepaper. Untold thousands did home work in the meager apartments they shared with their families, producing clothing, placing snaps and buttons on cards, stringing rosary beads, setting stones in cheap jewelry, packaging shoelaces, and making artificial flowers, often for no more than five cents per hour.

Health was yet another factor in the development of middle-class attitudes about the working class and reform. At a time when antibiotics were unknown, few people were immunized for any diseases other than smallpox, pasteurized milk was not widely available, and refrigeration was unreliable at best. Preventing illness and recovering from injuries were often difficult. But the suffering did not affect all children equally. Infant and child mortality rates were higher in cities than in the country and higher among the poor than among the middle and upper classes. Crowded, drafty, and poorly ventilated apartments guaranteed that flu and other illnesses would ensnare entire families; inadequate sewers and garbage removal created breeding grounds for germ-carrying flies and mosquitoes; a rudimentary understanding of nutrition often led doctors to recommend only limited breast-feeding and mothers to regularly feed infants hard-to-digest meat, pickles, and other adult foods; and still-developing notions about infectious diseases and the "germ theory" led even respected pediatricians to prescribe cathartics like castor oil for diarrhea (just the opposite of the treatment necessary for the dehydration-causing digestive illnesses).

Although the statistics are sketchy—the Census Bureau did not begin collecting data on infant mortality until 1900, and then only in ten northern states and selected cities—infant and child mortality was very high at the turn of the century. More than 12 percent of children died before their first birthday, and another 5.7 percent died before they reached the age of five. (By comparison, the infant mortality rate in the United States for 2001 was less than 1 percent.) The most common causes of death, in order, were debility and injuries in newborns (at a time when postnatal care was extremely limited, premature births were a major problem), digestive illnesses, and respiratory problems. For children under the age of five, pneumonia and other respiratory ailments were responsible for a third of all deaths, and measles, scarlet fever, and diphtheria also killed many young children. These diseases—which are prevented by immunizations or cured with powerful drugs today—were virtually untreatable early in the twentieth century. Although all levels of society suffered from these childhood maladies, especially epidemics of diphtheria and flu that could flash through whole communities in a matter of days, the urban poor suffered the most. Studies completed in the early 1910s found that the infant mortality rate was 22 percent in families where the father's annual wages were less than $50 per family member, whereas it was "only" 6 percent in families where the breadwinner earned at least $400 per family member.

Middle-class reformers were horrified by these statistics, and they took note of the obvious differences between the conditions in which they lived and the conditions in which less fortunate Americans lived. Indeed, it is impossible to overestimate the influence of class on the Progressive reformers. They believed middle-class models of childhood and child rearing could—and should—be secured for all children, and tended to ignore cultural, economic, and religious differences in reaching their goals.

Affluent, compassionate Americans often referred to their poorer counterparts as "the other half." The phrase was made famous in Jacob Riis's 1890 book, *How the Other Half Lives,* a scathing description of the sad and debased lives of New York City's neediest residents. (The title comes from an old English saying that "one half of the world does not know how the other half lives.") The phrase also appeared in the headline of a *Chicago Tribune* article about the Child Welfare Exhibit: "Crystallizing Theories into Simple Facts at the Welfare Exhibit, That the First Half May Know How the Other Half Lives." The reporter described the middle and upper-class women—with their "soft voice[s]" and "gay silk dress[es]" arguing about milk and nutrition with the dozens of poor mothers—"shabby, bareheaded except for an occasional shawl over their heads"—clustered around the booth. At first, wrote the reporter, the poor women resisted the notion that beer and cabbage were not appropriate foods for babies. But they changed their minds after seeing waxen models of sickly and healthy children, after reading information about the benefits of drinking milk, and after hearing "sharp" words from the well-to-do demonstrator. The article stated confidently that none of the women who visited

 Jacob Riis (1849—1914), a Danish immigrant, prowled the slums of New York as a journalist and photographer No one knew more about the city's mean streets than Riis, and he exposed that awful knowledge in hundreds of photographs and several books. In How the Other Half Lives, published in 1890, Riis tries to reveal to the wealthier "half of the population how the poorer half lives. As an immigrant himself, and as a passionate critic of the economic and political systems that allowed poor, immigrant neighborhoods to deteriorate and fester, Riis was more interested in exposing the terrible living conditions in the ethnic slums than in blaming the residents for their shortcomings.

Jacob Riis, How the Other Half Lives (New York: Charles Scribners Sons, 1890, 1901; New York: Dover Publications, 1971) 137—43.

Author's Note:
The Reverend Endicott Peabody and Jacob Riis knew each other. An excerpt from one of E.P's letters reads as follows:

May 16, 1896- Riis [Jacob Riis] wrote me the other day that his little child said as she looked at the Sunset "God can paint good, can't he Mamma" and that is the kind of feeling that filled ones heart. If heaven is more beautiful what a glorious place it will be! My mind is not quite free from care tonight. For two boys have measles with temperatures of over 104° and I am a little afraid of pneumonia. But I trust that it may be averted. - E.P.[1]

---

[1] From *Peabody of Groton* by Frank D. Ashburn

that booth "will ever feed beer to a baby again."

HOW THE OTHER HALF LIVES

Although "the other half" was, of course, simply a metaphor, Progressives were serious about studying the lives of poor Americans and creating programs to assist them. In fact, a hallmark of the Progressive approach was a compulsion to do research, to identify and articulate problems before developing solutions. Perhaps nothing reflected the middle-class assumptions of child welfare reformers—and their attitudes about the proper relationships between parents and children and the best ways for children to spend their leisure time—than the numerous studies they conducted on child labor. The most popular subjects of their research were newsboys. Reformers conducted at least sixteen studies of newsboys (sometimes including other street traders), in cities such as New York, Cincinnati, Dallas, and Milwaukee, between 1910 and 1925. Although thousands of children worked in southern mills (in small towns or rural areas), in northern sweatshops, and in tenement apartments, doing "home work" with their parents, one of the most prominent faces of child labor for urban Americans was the ubiquitous newsboy. From the 1850s through the 1920s newsboys were responsible for selling millions of newspapers each day. Their romantic, carefree lives were celebrated in dime novels and movies. Even reformers admitted that it was sometimes hard to get the public to understand that newsboys and other street traders were not simply spunky entrepreneurs, but child laborers with little control over their work. Although a majority of newsboys actually lived with their parents, they nevertheless became the symbol of city children who were denied the kind of childhoods that middle-class reformers believed every child had the "right" to enjoy. They also showed how easy it was for boys to slip into a world of dissolution and crime, which could lead to serious problems for the entire society. "If we do not lift him up," wrote one anxious organizer of newsboys, "he will pull us down."

The concern with the moral development of children emerged in another set of studies on how boys and girls spent their leisure time. In reports based on interviews with juvenile delinquents, surveys of school children, and the comments of teachers, social workers, and parents, researchers in cities as small as Springfield, Illinois, and as large as Cleveland and Los Angeles, found that the lack of recreational options led children to inappropriate behavior and even to crime. Studies presented vignettes of boys and girls idling away their time and, in many cases, descending into juvenile delinquency. A Cleveland boy interviewed at the State Industrial School claimed that he spent at least eleven hours a day "in the streets", at the movies, in the railroad yards, and at the athletic club—actually a pool hall. He also liked going to burlesque shows for the "good jokes" and dancing, and to a local amusement park. Without a neighborhood playground or baseball team, he turned to petty thievery, breaking into freight cars and stealing fruit and, in one escapade, ten cases of ginger ale. His first trip to the State Industrial School was for chronic truancy, being "a general nuisance in the neighborhood"; the second was for breaking into cars. That this boy was out of control seemed confirmed by his statement,

Florence Kelley

Among the many famous and powerful women whose names are associated with the Settlement House movement and the Progressive movement of the early 20th Century, one of the most remarkable was Florence Kelley. Yet, Kelley's name and her wide range of contributions to social reform and social justice are not as frequently remembered as are those of some her associates and fellow reformers, such as Julia Lathrop or Lillian Wald. Kelley's role in the abolishment of child labor, the passage of protective legislation for working women, the establishment of minimum wage laws, and the development of maternal and child health services qualify her for recognition as a seminal force in American life. (Goldmark, 1953, p. 2).

Kelly coined a phrase that became a motto for other child and youth advocates during this period and beyond. She asserted that Americans must mobilize to protect a right to childhood, thus defining a special and new way to look at the early years of a person's life.

Young Girl working in a Boston mill

"My people never knew, when I left home in the morning, whether I was going to school or not." All of this had happened before he turned fifteen. The inadequacy of recreational facilities—and of children's awareness of even the meager facilities that were available—was highlighted in the story of an eleven-year-old girl who "never drew books from the library, never used playgrounds, and did not know what a park looked like." She was in court because of her relationship with men who worked at the railroad freight yard. The men gave the girl and her friends toys, candy, money, and coal (for their families) in return for unnamed favors. When the girl was asked how often she went to the woods, she replied, "I don't know what a woods is.

Progressives also established a number of associations that published journals on the specific needs of children and youth. Reflecting the movement's commitment to the professionalization of child welfare, these organizations and the journals they published included the New York Charity Organization Society (COS), whose *Charities and the Commons* covered a wide variety of reforms and activities from all over the country; the Federated Boys' Clubs, *Work with Boys,* a report of the activities and projects carried out by Boys Clubs around the country; the Playground Association of America, *The Playground;* the National Congress of Mother's (later the Parent Teacher Association), *Child Welfare* magazine; and the National Child Labor Committee's, *Child Labor Bulletin.*

Reformers regularly held conferences—the most prominent was the annual National Conference on Charities and Corrections on health and legal issues, playground development, nutrition, and education. Settlement houses like Hull House sponsored workshops for welfare workers and parents alike, and the General Federation of Women's Clubs and the National Congress of Mothers advocated for more federal support of children's issues. In 1911 New York City and Chicago hosted well-attended child welfare exhibits on the problems facing children and ways to solve them. The federal government's increasing involvement in children's issues was the White House Conference on Dependent Children, called by President Theodore Roosevelt and held in Washington early in 1909. Attended by more than two hundred child welfare experts, the two-day meeting examined the problems facing children, discussed possible solutions, and declared that the twentieth century would be the century of the child.

The men and women who founded these organizations, attended their conferences, and wrote for their publications were professional journalists, social workers, and experts in a number of fields related to urban life. A modern American might call them "policy wonks" who had broken free from the amateur, religious-oriented reformism of the nineteenth century. They were less judgmental than their counterparts in previous generations, more interested in the well-being than the souls of the people they were trying to help, and dedicated to bringing private and public resources at the local, state, and federal levels to bear on social problems.

A RIGHT TO CHILDHOOD
Florence Kelley, an advocate for children at the turn of the century, coined a phrase in 1905

Orphan Trains

—*These waifs, human driftwood thrown up by a great city*—
Charles Loring Brace (1826-1890)

that became another motto for advocates for youth during this period and beyond when she asserted that Americans must mobilize to protect "a right to childhood." Of course, there had always been informal private, limited efforts to help children. Cities often held "poor children's days," treating newsboys, residents of orphanages, and other underprivileged children to a parade, free food, and entertainment. In 1893, hundreds of children paraded through downtown Chicago, crowded onto a train that took them to a field on the South Side, feasted and played games, and finished the day by attending a special performance of Buffalo Bill's "Wild West Show." The reform-minded magazine *The Delineator* took on the plight of orphaned and abandoned children in 1907 with its Child-Rescue Campaign, in which the magazine published adorable pictures and glowing descriptions of small children currently living in institutions who were available for adoption. Prior to the Gilded Age and the Progressive Era, child welfare issues were addressed by private institutions or individuals rather than local, state, or federal governments. These private efforts continued in the twentieth century. There were 1,151 institutions for dependent children in the United States in 1910; most were supported by private societies or religious denominations, which often "placed out" the children to shops, factories, or farms. The late nineteenth and early twentieth centuries also saw the heyday of the famous "orphan trains," sponsored by Charles Loring Brace's New York based Children's Aid Society. From the 1850s to the 1920s, these trains carried as many as 150,000 urban children to live with western families. As private efforts on behalf of the least fortunate city dwellers grew, public contributions dwindled. During the twenty years before 1900, city governments slashed or eliminated entirely their budgets for "outdoor relief"—the only direct aid to poor residents living outside poorhouses, county farms, and other institutions for the temporary housing of the poor.

Despite this retrenchment by city governments, some states became increasingly involved in the care of poor children, foreshadowing the more active government programs that developed after 1930. After the Civil War, most northern state governments housed orphans and so-called "half orphans" (children who had lost a mother or a father) of Union veterans at soldiers' orphans' homes. While most of these homes closed in the 1870s and 1880s, a few—notably in Illinois and Indiana—branched out to become the primary state-funded institutions for dependent children. The federal government also made tentative efforts to help the children of Union veterans with a system of widows and orphans pensions.

Progressives targeted most aspects of children's lives. The campaigns that were most relevant to urban youth addressed children's health, juvenile justice, and child labor issues. Nineteenth century reformers had initiated a number of efforts on behalf of urban children, from the Children's Aid Societies that sought homes for orphaned or needy children to the Societies for the Prevention of Cruelty to Children that were first organized in American cities in the 1870s.

Also confronting the effect of urban poverty on children were the settlement houses that began appearing in American cities in the late 1880s. In 1889, Jane Addams founded one of the first settlement houses in the United States in an old mansion on Chicago's West Side. She and her

*1889-Jane Addams and Ellen Gates Starr found Hull House,
the famous social settlement on the West Side of Chicago.*

partner, Ellen Gates Starr, named their settlement Hull House. Although it was not primarily aimed at children, because of the large concentration of young people in the immigrant neighborhoods surrounding it, it became a center of child welfare efforts in Chicago. Indeed, Addams used Hull House as the base of operation for her leadership in a number of reform efforts, from regulation of child labor to the passage of compulsory education laws. Hull House was a pioneer in other quieter, smaller child welfare efforts. For instance, it organized a kindergarten in the 1890s and in 1893 Chicago's first public playground. Over the years its clubs, rural camps, child care programs, and other services for the young became extremely popular. The settlement house movement expanded rapidly, until by 1910 there were more than 400 settlements around the country.

The settlement houses were, in many ways, the precursors of most Progressive Era child welfare reforms. Many settlement house programs were related to the health of children, one of the most important priorities for urban Progressives. Progressives initiated a number of medical and educational programs revolving around prenatal, infant, and child care. Departments of health in a number of cities sent visiting nurses into slum neighborhoods, set up aid stations (sometimes called "baby tents") to provide clean, well-ventilated, temporary child care, and instructed young girls in nutrition, personal hygiene, and rudimentary child development as part of the so-called Little Mothers' Movement.

The culmination of the campaign to utilize the resources of the federal government to address children's health issues was the creation of the United States Children's Bureau within the Department of Commerce and Labor in 1912. Julia C. Lathrop was named first head of the agency, and although she had a tiny budget (only $25,000 in the first year) and a small staff, over the next thirty years the bureau—first federal agency in the world dedicated to children—conducted research on child labor and health issues, published pamphlets on child rearing and nutrition, and sponsored events celebrating infant and children's health. One of the bureau's successes was convincing Congress to pass the Sheppard-Towner Act in 1921, which appropriated $7 million to establish local departments of maternity and infant hygiene. During its first three decades of existence, the bureau published scores of studies on child care, child health, and child labor. Some historians of the bureau, however, are critical of its focus on a narrowly middle-class set of values and assumptions and on its framing of child welfare as a "woman's issue." These approaches, as well as the failure of the federal government to support its programs with adequate resources, hindered the effectiveness of the bureau and made its eventual absorption into other federal agencies inevitable.

Despite its limited accomplishments, the bureau was an important source of information about children's health. Reformers had long believed that one of the greatest causes of poor health among infants and children was ignorance, especially among poor, immigrant groups whose child-rearing practices were patterned after traditional approaches that had long been discredited by science. The bureau initiated baby week campaigns, providing flyers, publicity, how-to bulletins, posters, and other items to state and local organizations. Organizations including public health departments, the Camp Fire Girls, agricultural college extension services, women's groups, hospitals, county governments, churches, and chambers of commerce sponsored baby week events. Generally held in the spring, the events varied dramatically from community to community, but generally included exhibits, lectures, stereopticon displays, and demonstrations on nutrition, the importance of pasteurized milk, creating healthy environments (with adequate ventilation and screened windows, for instance), vaccinations, clothing, and traffic safety. Many baby weeks included competitions for the best slogans, most creative posters and poetry, and essays on child health. Some held "better mothers" contests whose winners earned the best score on child care examinations. Some gave awards to the healthiest babies, who were presented at festive pageants and featured in laudatory newspaper articles. Indeed, the baby contests became one of the most popular—and, because of their exploitive nature, controversial—parts of the campaign.

Progressive efforts to improve public health clearly had humanitarian motives. Juvenile delinquency, the second major concern of child welfare reformers in turn-of-the-century cities, inspired not only compassion for youths, but also fear for the safety of the larger society Emerging ideas about delinquency and juvenile justice were part of a larger movement to force society as a whole to take responsibility for crime and to allow the expanding court system, particularly low-level municipal courts, to "manage" minor crimes and civil cases. The rising interest in the plight of delinquents led to a wide-ranging battery of reforms, from juvenile courts to organized playgrounds to Boys Clubs. Although the concern about delinquency centered on a criminal justice system that treated young defendants and convicts the same way it treated adults, reformers actually created a coherent program designed to prevent delinquency as well as to rehabilitate juveniles after they ran afoul of the law. Many of these programs reflected the middle-class assumptions that shaped other campaigns. The programs also generally ignored girls, regarding delinquency as the "boy problem." One particular reform that did affect girls was related to a concern over the moral development of juvenile boys: between the 1880s and 1920 every state of the union raised the age of consent from between ten or twelve years to sixteen or eighteen years of age.

The link between delinquency and spare time—made explicit in the studies of how children and youth spent their leisure time—was an important subtext in the playground movement that began in the 1880s and 1890s. The playground movement was responsible for the creation of local associations that hired supervisors for school playgrounds during the summer months, published guides to group games and activities, formed baseball teams, created ice skating rinks and sand piles, and lobbied schools and cities to include recreational facilities in their budgets. Numerous organizations participated in the playground movement, including settlement houses, the Woman's Christian Temperance Union, and women's clubs. In Philadelphia the Culture Extension League, the Civic Club, and the City Park Association all took part. An Outdoor Recreation League was formed in New York City, where in 1898 the school board opened two dozen school playgrounds during the summer under the supervision of 153 directors and assistants. By 1908, reported *Charities and the Commons,* 185 cities maintained supervised playgrounds, two-thirds of them funded by local governments. The professionalization of recreation and play was an important part of the playground movement. In addition to publishing a journal, the Playground Association of America held periodic "play congresses," where delegates discussed and held workshops on funding, the training of supervisors, the design of parks and play apparatus, the organization of day camps and excursions for children, the effect of organized play and playgrounds on juvenile delinquency, and efforts to pass laws regulating playgrounds and recreational facilities.

Both boys and girls benefited from the playground movement, but boys remained the chief target for reformers concerned with the lack of good recreational options. "The boy problem is one of the most important and most difficult problems of the present," wrote one observer. "Crowded cities and specialized industrial work have deprived the boy of opportunities for healthful play and wholesome occupation. The street and the alley have become his playground and his lounging place; the pool-room, the cigar-store and a saloon are open to receive him. Our cities have developed without reference to existence or the needs of the boy—the man of the next generation." This attitude inspired a massive effort to solve the "boy problem," which was actually a number of problems: delinquency, lack of affordable recreational facilities, crowded homes, neglectful parents, and the boundless energy of youth.

Boys Clubs became one of the most popular efforts to shape city boys. Several women organized the first club in Hartford, Connecticut, in 1860, but the idea didn't actually take hold until the 1890s. In 1906, the Federated Boys Clubs was formed in Boston with 53 member organizations. Although the clubs frequently offered courses in handicrafts, art, and even English, their primary purpose was to provide safe, wholesome, and supervised recreation. Clubs sponsored baseball teams, held summer camps, provided gymnasiums, and organized outings. In addition, the boys were encouraged to develop a community spirit reflected in the names they chose for themselves: "The Lily Club," "The Yellow Kids," "The Cuban Avengers," "Success Club," "Young Americans," "Loyalty Club," "The Pilgrims," "North Side Boys' Club," and "Clean Street Aids."

Many of the new institutions created for children and youth introduced a limited form of self-government. The most famous was William R. George's "Junior Republic," established in the mid-1890s near Freeville, New York. Guided by the motto "Nothing without labor," the boys (and, later, girls) brought to Freeville by distressed parents or sent there by juvenile court judges lived and worked with adult supervision and discipline. But they also elected dozens of their own representatives, earned money to spend at the republic shop (the republic even produced its own currency for a number of years), and agreed to follow rules established by their elected representatives and judges, to the extent that they could be fined or even sentenced to "jail" for infractions. The Junior Republic normally housed teenagers, but much younger boys, eight to thirteen years old, resided at the "Commonwealth of Ford"—also known as the Ford Republic—outside Detroit. The boys elected to official positions received salaries and

Photo by Lewis Hine

status in the community. A thirteen-year-old Ford Republic "judge" became a local celebrity in Detroit, and when he died tragically from a heart ailment the state supreme court sent one of its members to the funeral. The commitment to boys' self-government in the institution became a model for dozens of similar organizations, including the United States of Tacoma in Washington State; the "State of Columbia," established by a boys club in San Francisco; the Boys' Brotherhood Republic in Chicago, which established its own savings bank and employment agency; and "newsboys' republics," created in Milwaukee, Toledo, and other cities, which elected officers, helped regulate newsboys' work, sponsored sports teams and other activities, and, in Milwaukee, published a newspaper.

Organizations like the Boy Scouts, the Girl Scouts, and the Camp Fire Girls also promoted middle-class ideas and provided wholesome entertainment, taught useful skills, and insured appropriate supervision by adults. The "guardian" of the Cleveland Park Camp Fire in Washington D.C., reported a wide array of educational and recreational activities for the second half of 1912. In addition to swimming, tennis, roller skating, "outdoor sleeping," and singing, the girls received first-aid and embroidery lessons; heard lectures on hygiene, book illumination, and birds; and visited a book bindery, the U.S. Bureau of Standards, a bakery, and the city's filtration plant and pumping station. These outings were not simply for fun; hour-long examinations followed lectures on subjects like "The Proper Disposal of Waste and Garbage."

The first Boy Scout handbook described the "virtues" that members should learn and reflect: the "Twelve Points of the Scout Law." A Boy Scout must be trustworthy, loyal, helpful, friendly, courteous, kind, obedient, cheerful, thrifty, brave, clean, and reverent. None of these qualities appeared in contemporary descriptions of newsboys, street urchins, "dependent" children, or desperately poor immigrant youth. In a way, the scouting movement was designed to shape children to be just the opposite of what many activists believed to be the typical city child. One leading historian of the Boy Scouts and other "character-building agencies" argues that, although inspired by the public image of urban children as delinquents in training, local and national Boy Scout leaders—drawn from the middle class—worked harder to recruit boys from their own class than to recruit poor, immigrant children from the cities. Despite the fairly narrow goals and attitudes animating character building—or, perhaps, because of them—these groups were wildly popular. There were well over 400,000 Boy Scouts by the early 1920s."

Some new organizations sought simply to bring at-risk city children into contact with responsible, adult role models. The Big Brothers and Big Sisters both emerged in the early 1900s, and a short-lived "Caddy Camp" brought a few dozen city boys to a golf resort in the White Mountains of New Hampshire, where they camped out and caddied for wealthy, active men. The idea behind the caddy camp was that the boys would absorb the men's work ethic and other useful values. Similarly, the Wisconsin Home and Farm School aimed to prevent delinquency by taking troubled boys out of the city—mostly from nearby Milwaukee—and teaching them to become good citizens through hard work, close supervision, and tough but loving care. Scores of groups with similar goals emerged around the nation during this period.

Of course, not all city boys and girls had access to such organizations, and some simply refused to take part. Turn of the century Americans believed that something had to be done about juvenile delinquency, especially among boys. One of the most enduring examples of Progressive efforts to balance responsibility with compassion, to distinguish between youth and adults, and to put the government to work on behalf of young people was the establishment of separate court systems for juveniles. Throughout the 1880s and 1890s there had been efforts to ease the treatment of young criminals: The state of Massachusetts held separate hearings for children, some young offenders were put on probation rather than sent to jail, and in a few cities philanthropic organizations organized jailhouse schools for incarcerated youths.

Although the best-known advocate of juvenile courts early in the century was the Denver judge Benjamin Lindsey, women's club members, settlement house workers, and social scientists—united by gender, middle-class assumptions, and a desire to soften juvenile justice with a strong dose of maternalism—led the turn of the century drive to establish juvenile courts. Female advocates were more willing than their male counterparts to stress the importance of protecting innocent children over protecting society from delinquents. They were also more likely than men to insist on establishing new laws and courts rather than simply work within the existing criminal justice system. Most states adopted their approach; the first court devoted solely to juveniles was created in Chicago in 1899, and by 1920 virtually every state in the union had passed laws establishing special courts, probation systems, and detention homes for juvenile offenders.

The goal of these courts, according to Lindsey, was to defend "the sacred period of adolescence." Reformers believed that treating youthful criminals as adults ignored the social, economic, and cultural causes of their behavior. Moreover, sending them to jail only brought them into contact with hardened adult offenders and inevitably corrupted youths even further. Juvenile court judges, like Lindsey, treated delinquents on a case-by-case basis, weighing the conditions in which they had been raised against the crimes they were accused of committing. Jail sentences were rare; judges tried to counsel the youth who came before them, put them on probation in the custody of a responsible adult, or, if institutionalization was necessary, send them to a reform school rather than jail. An important distinction made by these reform-minded jurists was the difference between a delinquent and a criminal. The former, they believed, could be rehabilitated if treated correctly. Although juvenile courts were publicized as great child-saver success stories, the facts were more complicated. Critics of the system have accused juvenile courts of being more interest in controlling city youth than in bringing them to justice. In many cases, the "delinquents" brought before the courts had been arrested for activities that were not crimes. A 1913 study of an immigrant neighborhood in New York City revealed that more than half of juvenile arrests were for "begging, bonfires, gambling, jumping on [street]cars, ... playing with water pistols, putting out lights, selling papers, shooting craps, snowballing, subway disturbances, and throwing stones." Boys and girls alike were brought before juvenile courts on vague charges like "incorrigibility," "immorality," and disorderly conduct. Some parents and teachers simply used the new courts as a way to get troublesome teenagers out of their classrooms and off the street, at least temporarily.

Another major priority for Progressives was the campaign against child labor, which became one of the movement's largest efforts. Throughout the nineteenth century, trade unions had advocated restrictions on child labor, arguing that work deprived children of equal access to education and that the low wages paid to children depressed the wages of working adults. Late in the 19th century the National Consumers League took the lead in the fight against child labor, but many other humanitarian and philanthropic organizations—church groups, women's clubs, settlement houses, and social service organizations—joined the fight. By the turn of the century, child labor committees had been formed in New York, Alabama, and several other states, and by 1903 a number of states had passed significant child labor legislation.

When leaders of these committees and organizations decided to agitate for a national approach to child labor, they formed the National Child Labor Committee (NCLC) in 1904. The NCLC worked to mobilize the public, labor unions, and politicians against child labor. Although it did not focus, strictly speaking, on city children, the NCLC drew much of its support from urban child welfare workers. Its publications highlighted the damage that full-time work could do to children, including lost limbs, respiratory diseases, bent backs, and undeveloped minds. Through investigations and publicity garnered by the work of pioneering photographers like Lewis Hine, the NCLC promoted the enforcement of existing child labor laws and the passage of stricter regulations. The model law promoted by the NCLC was fairly weak by twenty-first-century standards: a minimum age of fourteen for working in factories, and sixteen in mines; an eight-hour day for fourteen- and fifteen-year-old industrial workers; and no night work for youths under the age of sixteen. The resulting Keating-Owen Act of 1916 carried great symbolic value—it incorporated most NCLC goals—but applied to only a fraction of the children employed in the United States. Many southerners opposed the law because it gave the federal government power over the states. Others fought against it because they believed children were better off working in factories than idling on the streets, and that until there were enough schools for youth to attend—southern states lagged far behind northern states in providing postelementary education for their children—they should continue working. The U.S. Supreme Court ruled the Keating-Owen Act unconstitutional only nine months after passage. Effective federal regulation of child labor would not be implemented until the Fair Labor Standards Act of 1938.

CULTURES OF CHILDREN AND YOUTH

The story of the child in the city would not be complete without the children's own perceptions of city life. As in so many other facets of children's lives, class differences led to the creation of a number of separate cultures of children and youth. One form of youth culture centered in the burgeoning high schools. The first American high school, Boston English, was established in 1821. The number of high schools in the United States grew slowly throughout the nineteenth century, and although the percentage of teenagers in high school remained relatively small, the number of high schoolers increased dramatically during the late nineteenth and early twentieth centuries, from 72,000 in 1870 to more than two million in 1920. Perhaps a third of all fourteen- to seventeen-year-olds attended high school in 1920, and approximately 16 percent actually graduated. Middle and upper-class boys and girls (in fact, girls constituted a substantial majority of most graduating classes during this time) were far more likely to attend high school than working-class, immigrant, and African American students, although high schools nevertheless became the center of a developing youth culture.

Students established sports teams and debating societies, published school newspapers and yearbooks, ran student governments, and organized dances and other social events. Over time, school administrators took control over most student activities in American high schools, establishing conferences for sports teams, requiring coaches, conductors, and other advisers of student activities to be faculty members, limiting participation in official activities (especially sports) to students in good academic standing, and censoring student publications. They created regulated, safe and structured places that could not have been more different from the wild and woolly environment of the streets.

Only a small minority of teenagers actually attended school, however, and another form of youth culture also flourished on city streets which became playgrounds for stickball, marbles, hide-and-seek, and various improvised street games. The crowded working-class and immigrant neighborhoods became communities of children, where older siblings watched out for and trained younger children; where games with elaborate rules evolved; where "turf" wars between children of various ethnic groups were common; where dead horses, fires, fights, and accidents provided street drama; where discarded objects became improvised toys—bicycle wheels turned into hoops, bags full of rags into footballs, garbage-pail lids into sleds. Girls claimed the stoops in front of tenements as their territory, where they played house (often while taking care of younger brothers and sisters), and boys owned the streets where they competed for space with carriages, street merchants' carts, streetcars, and pedestrians. And every block or two they could find a place where, for a few cents, they could watch a scratchy, soundless movie.

Two archetypal city boys represent these two vastly different youth cultures. Claude G. Bowers, who as an adult would be a well-known newspaper editor and columnist, historian, Democratic party leader, and ambassador to Spain and Chile, attended Shortridge High School in Indianapolis in the 1890s. Claude kept a detailed diary with nearly daily reports of his club and class activities. He and his friends were constantly on the go, attending lectures at local colleges and at the high school (speakers included Jane Addams and Booker T. Washington), playing poker, attending the opera and theater, and sightseeing in nearby villages. But Claude and his friends had time for school events, too, and his diary frequently mentions politicking for class offices, formal school debates, the publication of a school literary magazine and yearbook, mock trials, reading clubs, the formation of an oratorical association (he was elected president), the school's annual "Puritan supper" (a kind of Thanksgiving celebration), and other intellectual and social pursuits. He also managed to find time for girls, reporting late in his senior year that he and a friend "once more had engagements with the girls of the Spooners Club, and had a great time as usual, 50 kisses, 3 girls on lap, 25 embraces. Ye Gods! and still we live." In New York, at about the same time, a little Jewish boy entered the youth culture of the streets. Adolph "Harpo" Marx, who would become the white-wigged, horn-honking but otherwise silent member of the Marx Brothers comedy team, was one of those turn-of-the-century street kids about whom reformers worried so much. Harpo and his brothers Chico and Groucho virtually lived on the streets of New York. School was not a priority of the Marx brothers, who spent their time scrounging for money, gambling, and battling the Irish, German, and Italian boys whose neighborhoods bordered their own Upper East Side Jewish enclave.

"It was all part of the endless fight for recognition of foreigners in the process of becoming Americans," Harpo recalled many years later. "Every Irish kid who made a Jewish kid knuckle under was made to say 'Uncle' by an Italian, who got his lumps from a German kid, who got his insides kicked out by his old man for street fighting and then went out and beat up an Irish kid to heal his wounds." When the boys were not fighting each other, they were cutting a wide swath through the neighborhoods. "Individually and in gangs," Harpo recalled, "we accounted for most of the petty thievery and destruction of property on the Upper East Side," and, as a result, they were "hounded," "harassed," and "chased" by police officers, who "every chance they got, happily beat the hell out of us."

Harpo spent a lot of time in Central Park, searching for lost tennis balls, "sledding" in wintertime on stolen dishpans, and ice skating on a single hand-me-down skate. He also described swimming amid the floating garbage in the East River, making "snazzy" rings out of hairs yanked from brewery horses' tails, "swindling" ticket takers on the "el" in order to get to the Polo Grounds, where he could watch baseball games for free from a bluff overlooking left field (which was, unfortunately, the only part of the field he could see). The family splurged one day each year on an excursion to North Beach in the Bronx. Family members swam, sunbathed, ate watermelon, played in the sand, told jokes, and generally forgot their cares until catching the last ferry home. "It was always a melancholy homecoming," because everyone knew that it would be another year before they could once again leave behind the "hard work and misery" that characterized every other day of the year.

Both Claude and Harpo grew up to lead successful adult lives. But their vastly different backgrounds not only represent the wide range of childhood experiences of Americans in the late nineteenth and early twentieth century—and only the experiences of white males from northern cities—but also suggest some of the differences in perceptions and assumptions of middle-class and working-class Americans. Claude was sophisticated, calm, urbane, a follower of rules who embraced typical ambitions and values. Harpo was a shrewd hustler bent on testing boundaries. Youths like Harpo made adult versions of Claude nervous, but also inspired them to undertake humane, if flawed, efforts to improve the lives of disadvantaged urban children and youth. That tension lies at the center of Childhood and Child Welfare in the Progressive Era.

A Chronology of Child Welfare Reforms
(1853-1938)

1853	Charles Loring Brace founds the Children's Aid Society in New York City.
1860	Reformers in Hartford, Connecticut, establish the first Boys Club.
1867	The first installment of Horatio Alger's first rags-to-riches story begins running in *The Student and Schoolmate*. It was later published as *Ragged Dick*, or, *Street Life in New York*.
1870	U.S. Census first records child labor.
1872	Charles Loring Brace publishes *The Dangerous Classes of New York, and Twenty Years' Work among Them*, a memoir of his work in New York's slums.
1874	New York Society for the Prevention of Cruelty to Children is established. New York City Department of Health distributes infant care and diphtheria leaflets.
1878	First free kindergarten in the East founded in New York City.
1888	American Pediatric Association founded.
1889	Jane Addams and Ellen Gates Starr found Hull House, the famous social settlement on the West Side of Chicago.
1892	Jacob Riis, the photographer and social reformer, publishes *The Children of the Poor*, an exposé of the harsh living conditions of children in the ghettos of New York City. John Gunckel establishes the Toledo Newsboys' Association, one of the most successful organizations of its type in the country.
1893	Lillian Wald establishes the Henry Street Settlement in Lower Manhattan. Rev. Endicott Peabody and brethren establishes the first summer camp for "Underprivileged" boys on Squam Lake, N.H.; "Groton School Camp."[1]
1894	The Child Study Association begins applying social scientific research methods to the study of child development. Boston begins requiring medical inspections of school children. Luther Emmett Holt publishes *The Care and Feeding of Children*, one of the most popular "modern" child-rearing guides.
1895	William George establishes the first junior republic, a self-governing camp for city youth, at Freeville, near Ithaca, New York.
1899	The first juvenile court in the United States is established in Chicago. Connecticut is the first state to require medical inspections and eye tests of children.
1900	About 8 percent of all children in the United States between the ages of 14 and 17 attend high school. The Swedish author and educator Ellen Key publishes *The Century of the Child*.

---

[1] *Included by Editor*

1902	New York City begins the first school nursing program.
1904	The National Child Labor Committee, the first effective lobbying group for reforming child labor conditions, is established.
	G. Stanley Hall publishes the influential *Adolescence: Its Psychology and its Relations to Physiology, Anthropology, Sociology, Sex, Crime, Religion, and Education.*
1905	Florence Kelley publishes *Some Ethical Gains Through Legislation,* in which she declares that all children should have "a right to childhood."
	The first theater devoted solely to presenting moving pictures opens in Pittsburgh. Its first feature is *The Great Train Robbery.*
1906	The Federated Boys Clubs (later Boys Clubs of America and, later, the Boys and Girls Clubs of America) is formed. The Massachusetts legislature passes the nation's first school health law.
	Jacob Riis, Jane Addams, Lillian Wald, and others form the Playground Association of America.
1908	The Juvenile Protective Association is formed to promote juvenile courts, junior republics, and other child welfare activities.
	New York City establishes a child hygiene division in its city health department, the first in the United States.
	Boston establishes the first "fresh air" school for children suffering from tuberculosis and other respiratory problems.
1909	More than two hundred reformers attend a White House conference to discuss the care and management of the 150,000 orphaned and institutionalized children in the United States.
1910	New York City begins serving school lunches.
	The Boy Scouts of America is established.
	The Mann Act outlaws interstate transportation of girls and women for immoral purposes.
1911	The Camp Fire Girls is established.
	Illinois becomes first state to create pensions for widows with dependent children.
	The Safety Institute of America is founded. It publishes safety guides for adults and children, and lobbies for play grounds and other recreational opportunities for children.
	Child welfare exhibits are held in New York and Chicago.
1912	The U.S. Children's Bureau, the first federal agency devoted expressly to the welfare of children, is founded with Julia Lathrop as director. The Girl Scouts of America is established.
1916	The U.S. Congress passes and President Woodrow Wilson signs the Keating-Owens Act, the first federal legislation regulating child labor.
	Lewis Terman, a psychologist at Stanford, develops the intelligence quotient, a measurement of IQ that will be used to test children for decades.
1917	In Hammer v. Dagenhart, the U.S. Supreme Court declares the Keating-Owens Act unconstitutional.
1919	The White House Conference on Child Welfare Standards establishes standards for child employment, children's health and welfare, and medical care for infants and mothers.
1920	About 32 percent of all children between the ages of 14 and 17 attend high school.
1921	Congress passes the Sheppard-Towner Act, which provides for the gathering of statistics on prenatal care and infant mortality.

1922   The International Council of Women issues its Children's Charter, which proposes the development of a set of minimum rights for children throughout the world.

1930   Delegates to a White House conference issue the Children's Charter, a set of nineteen principles on health, education, child labor, recreation, and the family.

1938   President Franklin Roosevelt signs the Fair Labor Standards Act into law. It prohibits the employment of children under the age of 16.

From *CHILDHOOD AND CHILD WELFARE IN THE PROGRESSIVE ERA* by James Marten. Copyright © 2005. Used with permission by Bedford/St. Martin's Publishers.

Part II

HISTORY OF ORGANIZED CAMPING

IN THE UNITED STATES

—In the late nineteenth century the organized summer camp movement developed as a response to anxieties about the effects of the urban-industrial age on children.—
M. B. Smith

"A Good Time Coming" Currier & Ives

Chapter 2

History of Organized Camping

This chapter includes excerpts from "History of Organized Camping: The First Hundred Years" by Eleanor Eells. Reprinted with permission by the American Camping Association, Inc. Copyright © 1986. This section is not specific to the genesis of camping for the "underprivileged," but presented here to give insight into the camping movement as a whole.

ONE MIGHT WELL ASK THE QUESTION, why did organized camping spring up in the United States? And why at the particular time that it did? What were the social forces in America that led, late in the 1800's, to the development of what has become the organized camping movement?

Much of the frontier had disappeared. The westward movement had become a filling-in rather than a thrust to new areas. The industrial revolution had transformed an ever-increasing number of rural dwellers into urbanites. Many who had left the country for the cities deplored the complications of raising children in the crowded environment. A host of new institutions—settlement houses, youth organizations, public welfare and counseling agencies, and park and recreation agencies—all sought to provide for children something that seemed to be missing. Summer vacations from school, which children in an earlier rural society had spent in farm work, now called for an educational program that would escape the rigid discipline of the traditional schools. Organized camping, which offered city children experiences with open spaces and sunshine, seemed to be an answer.

ORGANIZED CAMPING, AN AMERICAN INSTITUTION

Most of the people of the United States have European backgrounds, and many of our institutions and methods of operation are naturally based on European concepts. There are many ideas, however, that originated and developed in the United States and have been exported

HISTORY OF ORGANIZED CAMPING

YMCA's Camp Dudley 1885. Longest continually run camp in the U.S.

Camp Dudley, Lake Champlain NY—c. 1895.

A pioneer of Organized Camping, the Y.M.C.A currently operates over 17,500 camps.

from our own country to the rest of the world. One of these, of special concern to us, is organized camping. As far as we know, there was no precedent in other countries for this program for youth. Admittedly young people had camped since the dawn of history; and many of the principles of group living and learning antedated the American organized camp. But the summer camp, as we know it, seemed to have developed in the United States. Outdoor living by young people in small groups within larger camp communities, isolated from city distractions, dedicated to free and joyous experiences with educational values, with leaders especially selected for their understanding and guidance skills: this is the American concept of camping. The ideal American camp provides an educational milieu that is one of the most favorable settings possible for helping young people to grow, develop, and achieve understanding of themselves and a sense of responsibility for others and for the environment.

INDIAN BACKGROUNDS

Those who explored, settled and exploited early America held an ambivalent attitude toward the American Indians. They feared and sometimes detested them. Conflict with the Indians was inevitable; the settlers came to establish their homes and to till land that they regarded as their own, whereas the Indians had no concept of or regard for individual land ownership.

At the same time, settlers found much to admire in Indian life. From the Indians they learned about the natural environment, new foods, and skills necessary to survival in the new world. They learned about the tribal councils, songs, dances, and traditions of bravery and fortitude. Indian belief in a Supreme Being struck a responsive chord among Christians. As conflicts with Indians receded, Indian life took its place in the lore of the past. It was perfectly natural that many early camps found a place in their programs for Indian traditions, names, challenges, and particularly the Indian council ring.

The organized camp in America bears the stamp of the westward movement. Romanticized legends and tales of the explorer, fur trader, trapper, settler, covered wagon pioneer, cowboy, and north woods logger have been woven into American art, music, and literature and have influenced the character of outdoor pursuits. Many early camps incorporated the flavor of the westward movement as well as Indian life and outdoor living into the very heart of their programs.

Camping as we know it in the United States today is a new phenomenon; whether it is a movement or an institution depends on one's point of view. It has become an important part of the American scene, rich in its diversity and in its adaptation to changing needs and challenges. Its common bond is the concern for people in their relationship to one another, to the environment, and for their sense of community.

Camping was the normal way of life in man's past, and there may be an element of nostalgia in the periodic return to the out-of-doors through individual family camping, backpacking and wilderness trips. Since two-thirds of the United States population of 220 million live in urban settings, the outdoor experience has become both necessary and satisfying.

1861-1910

In looking back, one can realize the impact of the Industrial Revolution, which resultred in the need for large number of workers in the cities. This increasing migration from farm to city, the successive waves of immigrants, the Civil War and the ensuing Reconstruction, economic booms and panics, Indian confrontations, and the Westward Trek for land and for gold, all

Gunnery School Camp, Connecticut, 1862
(Many consider this to be the first "Camp" in the U.S.)

contributed and influenced the development of social movements within the nation.

The modes and standards of the Victorian era and the Gilded Age were not marked by a tendency toward the natural, the primitive, or the unconventional; but they were in sharp contrast to the ideas of Rousseau, Thoreau, and the Romantic Movement. However, outing magazines flourished in the last half of the nineteenth century, and stories of adventure and of Indian and pioneer life fired the imaginations of city dwellers and conventional folk who seemed hungry for something beyond conservative Victorianism. The 1880s and 1890s saw many middle class families in the eastern part of the country living the simpler life in a cottage in the mountains or at a lake. The more affluent frequented the seashore and mountain resorts in preference to European tours. Educational opportunities increased; but they were organized to fit a conventional rigid structure and were available and suited primarily to the affluent youth. The mystique of nature and the appeal of the simple life influenced men and boys to explore the wilderness of the Northeast on foot and in canoes. They also took shorter trips, camping out in primitive fashion to experience the discipline of roughing it for at least a few days in the natural world. In such an atmosphere, resident youth camping was born. The pioneer heritage, the excitement over nature, the freer life styles, and the long school vacations all played a part; so did the church and private philanthropy, as men and women of conscience and good will struggled to understand and cope with burgeoning social problems. Camping played a conspicuous role as private enterprise, and, at its best, contributed to the needs of the affluent in one way and to the needs of the poor in another. The concept of two societies—one rich, one poor—was generally accepted as a successor to the simpler, more homogeneous society of the small American community. How does one date a beginning? Many writers refer to camping as old as man himself, and recalling the wanderings of the children of Israel; or Athens and Sparta educating the youth in the fields; or the primitive living of early settlers. Others specifically connect Indian life, or military encampments with the origins of organized camping.

ORGANIZED CAMPING

It is relevant to offer a description of camping here so that the reader may understand the similarities and differences between at least two forms of camping. To most people, "camping" means living out-of-doors or a form of housekeeping in a natural environment. It may suggest living in a tent, a cabin, sleeping on the ground under the stars, or even living in a motorized camper, recreation vehicle, or travel trailer. To camp implies participation in activities related to the natural resources such as hiking, fishing, cooking over a fire, building shelters, and erecting teepees or tents. Camping generally implies a way of life more simple than that to which the camper will return. Laundry, bathing, clothing, food, and personal amenities are simple, often primitive, in contrast to the home from which one came. This concept of camping occurs in small or large groups, often unsponsored by any organization; it is usually carried out for pure leisure or recreational purpose by groups of friends or relatives, with the leaders designated from within the group.

Organized camping on the other hand is defined as a "sustained experience which provides a creative, recreational, and educational opportunity in group living in the out-of-doors. It utilizes trained leadership and the resources of natural surroundings to contribute to each camper's mental, physical, social, and spiritual growth"

Organized camping is an enterprise sponsored by identifiable groups that recruit campers, provide living accommodations, and offer programs of educational and recreational intent under the leadership of people who have had training in the program, camper characteristics, safety, health and sanitation, and other facets of the operation. The sponsors are youth serving agencies, private corporations, individuals, churches, schools, and municipalities. The organized camping field is made up of day camps (from which campers return home each night), resident camps (at which campers stay for a period of several days, weeks, or perhaps months), and travel camps (which consist of campers moving to different sleeping sites each day through hiking, canoeing, riding or other means of travel). Somehow, the outdoors serves as a catalyst for group interaction which results in a well-being seldom found elsewhere. The trust generated between adults and youth and the feeling of accomplishment within the camper group is difficult to understand, and, thus far, difficult to verify through research. Whatever the combination of ingredients, something seems to happen at a camp that makes the campers feel good about themselves, about others, and about the environment in which they live. While it may be seen as an escape from the reality of urban life, it is also seen as a reaffirmation with the reality of compatible group living in a more natural community. Whatever it is, millions have been affected by an experience as youthful campers, and thousands of other young men and women have served as their counselors and leaders.

The definition of organized camping today does not appropriately describe the early private camps for teenage boys and girls in New England and the East, nor the many charitable camps which developed at relatively the same time. Still it is important to understand that all of these efforts were strands to be woven into the fabric of organized camping. All early leaders were concerned, in one way or another, with human needs, with the individual, with personal and group relationships, with a sense of community, and with the natural world and its Creator.

Eleanor Eells 1893-1987, Author, History of Organized Camping : The first 100 years.

Groton School Camp, Squam Lake NH. c.1890's

Part III

Groton School Camp History

—Ours was the first camp which enabled what is sometimes called the Underprivileged Boy to enjoy this sort of outdoor life equally with the more fortunate. — Rev. Endicott Peabody 1942

Groton School, Hundred House

Chapter 3

Groton Scholars Start A Camp

Rev. Endicott Peabody with wife Fannie

Tombstone—1882. The first Protestant Church in Arizona, for which Peabody raised the funds and was the first minister. .

—In 1892, Reverend Endicott Peabody presented the Camp idea to the Missionary Society of Groton School. The following summer Groton School Camp beacame a reality on Squam Lake NH. The following is a short bio of Mr. Peabody.

Reverend Endicott Peabody

THE REV. ENDICOTT PEABODY (30 May 1857—20 January 1944) was the American Episcopal priest who founded Groton School for Boys (known today simply as Groton School), in Groton, Massachusetts, in 1884. Peabody served as headmaster at Groton School from 1884 until 1940, and also served as a trustee at Lawrence Academy at Groton. Peabody was Franklin Delano Roosevelt's headmaster at Groton, and he officiated at FDR's marriage to Eleanor Roosevelt.

When Endicott Peabody was 13, the family moved to England. He prepared for university at Cheltenham College, a secondary school in Cheltenham, Gloucestershire, finishing in 1876 at the age of 19. He was graduated from Trinity College, Cambridge, in 1880 with an L.L.B. degree. He married his cousin, Fannie Peabody, daughter of Francis and Helen Peabody of Salem, Massachusetts on 18 June 1885 in Salem. They had six children.

Franklin Delano Roosevelt said of Peabody, "As long as I live his influence will mean more to me than that of any other people next to my father and mother." (As quoted in Peabody's obituary in the New York Times, April 13, 1944.)

In 1882 during his first year at the Episcopal Theological School in Cambridge, Massachusetts (now the Episcopal Divinity School) Peabody, a seminarian not yet a priest, was invited to take charge of a little Episcopal congregation in Tombstone, Arizona (now St. Paul's Episcopal Church, Tombstone). After a long and tortuous trip, Peabody arrived in Tombstone two months after the "Gunfight at OK Corral".

He had words of praise for Wyatt Earp. Though he spent no more than six months in Tombstone he succeeded in getting the church built that today is the oldest Protestant church in the state. He was impressive physically, never losing a boxing match. He began a baseball team in Tombstone. He raised money by walking into the saloons and holding out his hat at the gambling tables. He has been spoken of as patron saint of the Diocese of Arizona.

In 1892 he presented the Camp idea to the Missionary Society of Groton School which was enthusiastically accepted by all. The following summer Groton School Camp became a reality.

GROTON SCHOLARS START A CAMP

Above, Groton School Staff, 1890's. Many left the comfort of Groton to serve at the camp. Their pictures and log entries can be found throughout this book. First Row (lower step) L-R; N. Nichols, Abbott, Ogilby, Woods, Hinchman. Second Row; WAG*, Sturgis, Billings, Griswold, Higley, Richards. Third Row; Ayrault, Garrett, Moore, Gladwin, Jefferson, Cushing

* *WAG = William Amory Gardner*

The following is included to give the reader a sense of the quality of the Groton School staff that supported the Camp idea, and made it a reality. These are the types of people Groton School attracted before the turn of the century—and continues to attract this day.

"THERE CAN BE NO DOUBT that one of the main reasons for the success of Groton School was the caliber of its faculty.

During the first twenty-five years or so the average number of masters was not more than ten or twelve. Of Billings and Gardner more will be said later. Geddes went on to Boston University where he became a full professor. Higley, a real scholar, left Middlebury to come to Groton and remained until his death. Ayrault, Gladwin, Sturgis, Griswold, Abbott, Richards, Hinchman, Crane, Regan, Andrews, Call, Lynes, Jacomb, and later Thomas, Zahner, Nash, DeVeau stayed for more than twenty years; some of them for thirty, some for more than forty. Thayer left to be head of St. Mark's; Abbott of Lawrenceville. Cushing went into politics and became lieutenant governor of Massachusetts. Arthur Woods departed to be perhaps the best police commissioner New York ever had. Charles Slatterly became a bishop. Ellery Sedgwick was editor of the Atlantic Monthly. Julian Coolidge was one of the leading mathematicians at Harvard and master of Lowell House. Remsen Ogilby founded a school in the Philippines and later was president of Trinity College, Hartford.

Another thing that one must understand about Groton masters is that they belong to a calling. It was not exactly a profession, although the Rector always inculcated a sense of professional pride, because pedagogy was only part of their task. It was a calling. Of all the texts on which the Rector preached, the one he used most often, not only in the pulpit but in faculty meetings, was "For their sakes I sanctify myself"; and for a Groton master his job was not only a job, it was a way of life. It was not a way of life which would appeal to most men, because it meant giving up many pleasures and freedoms that most men value."[1]

---

[1] *From Peabody of Groton by Frank D. Ashburn. Used with permission.*

—Major Higley— sometimes called "The Walrus", "Tuskers" and the "Growler," on account of his long yellow moustache—but always kindly and loved by all—included here as representative of the caliber of the GS staff that supported the Camp idea.

Edwin H. Higley (1843-1916)

HIGLEY, EDWIN HALL, OF GROTON, MASS., son of Rev. Harvey O. and Sarah (Little) Higley, was born in Castleton, Vt., Feb. 15, 1843.

He received his preparatory education at Castleton Seminary, and then entered Middlebury College, where he graduated in the class of 1868. For the next four years he studied music and philology in Boston and Cambridge, and from 1882 to 1884 at the Royal Conservatory of Leipsic, in Germany.

Though scarcely emerged from boyhood, he was inspired with the enthusiasm attending the early outbreak of the war for the Union, and in 1861 he enlisted in Co. K, 1st Vt. Cavalry. During his service he was detailed as adjutant and as regimental commissary and in the latter part of 1863 acted as brigade ordnance officer on the staff of Gen. G. A. Custer. During Kilpatrick's raid he commanded a section of Battery C, 3d U. S. Artillery and had the satisfaction of shelling the rebel capitol. He was wounded and taken prisoner June 29, 1864, after having participated in most of the cavalry engagements of the Army of the Potomac in the campaigns of Pope, second Bull Run, Gettysburg and the Wilderness. Exchanged March 1, 1865, he was commissioned captain of Co. K, and soon after brevet major for gallant and meritorious service during the war.

From 1868 to 1872 Major Higley taught music in Boston, Mass., and then accepted a professorship of German and Greek in Middlebury College, where he remained ten years. After his return from Europe, he was teacher of music and organist in Worcester, Mass. In 1886 he went to Groton School as Greek and German instructor and as choir master and organist. He married Jane S. Oliver in 1870. They had one daughter—Margaret.

Major Higley—left of center— being rowed out to Groton School Camp.

The Main Camp Building

Mr. John Crocker & J. Shed. Crocker would later become headmaster of Groton School

Schenk, Nutter and Mr. Biddle

Mr. Richards at Ashland Train Station

GROTON SCHOLARS START A CAMP

T HE REGENERATION OF THE WORLD IS A KNOTTY PROBLEM which has vexed mankind and has given rise to many philosophies. Modern experience, the practical philosophy of the day, seems to teach that there is no short-cut to salvation and that the raising of mankind is a slow and tedious process which can be accomplished only by persistent work on the individual. The nursery rhyme has it that

> "Little drops of water,
> Little grains of sand,
> Make the mighty ocean,
> And the pleasant land."

and it is undoubtedly true that the ocean of reform, both political and social, will be the mass of the drops of small individual endeavor which are the characteristic sign of our modem civilization ....

G.D.C.[1]

Mr. Cushing at Camp.

[1] *Words From The 1901 Grotonian by faculty member Grafton D. Cushing, who later became Lt. Governor of Mass. (1915-16)*

Groton School Camp Staff

Well known Groton Staff Relaxing

Mr. Billings at camp

Gray, Addison, Schenck, Davis, Low, Nutter & Storer—c. 1907

Groton School Camp Staff; Top row L-R; B. Farr, Skinner, ladd, Mr. Sturgis Bottom L-R; Mr. Parsons, Edmonds, D. Dans, Mr. Mallison, Howard—1904

Groton School Camp Staff (Mr. Sturges 4th from left)—August 27, 1907

Mr. Thurston—later to became Episcopal Bishop of Oklahoma

Phil Smith

Mr. Higley at camp reading either Greek, German, Latin or English.

Mr. Biddle at desk in tent

GSC Staff; Stevie, C.R., & Potts—1907

—FOR 73 years—between 1893 and 1966—100's of Groton School staff and students gave up part of their summer to look after and guide thousands of campers— and thousands of donors stepped up to support them. It's impossible to include everyone here—but we are grateful to all who served.— KB

Images above are representative of the "underprivileged" child in the 1890s. In 1893, Groton School's Missionary Society established a camp to serve them - a first of its type. Images by Riis, Hine & Clyde B.

Chapter 4

Groton School Camp History (1)

A Reprint From The 1901 Grotonian

By:

S.S. Sturgis
G.D. Cushing
E.H. Higley

GROTON SCHOOL CAMP.
A Reprint From The 1901 Grotonian

OUR SUMMER CAMP AT LAKE ASQUAM has now grown old enough to have a history, as an institution which has passed through various periods of development and now bases its effective work upon the sure foundation of experience. The process of gathering that experience in the early days of the camp was very interesting and often exciting. Those were the good old days when "Merry Andrew" used to bite the holes in the doughnuts," and when the log recorded many an ingenious experiment with knotty problems. Yet camp life today has no lack of interest; and, moving smoothly along lines of well established tradition, carries with it far more influence upon the boys we entertain. A history of the camp should go back to an evening when Mr. Peabody first suggested such a work to the Missionary Society. That society greatly needed some field for active work, and warmly welcomed the new idea. This was in November of the year 1892, and before summer the difficult questions of location, putting up buildings and securing necessary funds, had been successfully met. In all the discussions of situation, of buildings needed, and of other practical details, Phil Smith and Julian Gerard, who had previously camped on Lake Asquam, were of immense assistance, and the former from that day to this has been architect, consulting engineer and head carpenter in all our

The kitchen crew at work

improvements. The camp was opened early in July, with Mr. Thurston as superintendent and Andrew Yonson as king of the kitchen, with only two buildings besides the faculty tents, with no play-house, no wharf, no infirmary, and, worst of all, no experience to guide us. I can answer for at least one 'senior member' of the faculty, who went to camp that first year with fear and trembling, and who daily dreaded a mutiny or a drowning accident. The season was, however, a decided success. We had about a hundred boys with us and many were the lessons we learned from and with them. I will not attempt to describe the separate years of camp history, but will briefly speak of a few ways in which the work has developed. First, in regard to material equipment. We now have two comfortable tents for the faculty, a large dormitory for the boys, a hexagonal dining hall with kitchen and pantry attached, a play-house for rainy weather, an infirmary, a good wharf and five boats. The grounds about the camp have been improved, a large space in the interior of the island has been cleared for a future play-ground, and a more convenient landing has been made upon the main land. Secondly, in regard to the financial support. This has come very largely from friends of the work who have subscribed ten dollars a year for a definite period of years. On one occasion also friends in New York arranged a concert in aid of the camp, and two years ago some ladies in New York raised money enough to pay almost the whole expense of the camp for the season. Control of the camp rests with a committee of five, composed of masters and boys of Groton School. The actual management during the summer devolves upon the resident superintendent, and in this position we have been fortunate in having such faithful and energetic helpers as Messrs. Thurston, Newbegin, Chauncey, Hawkins, Campbell and Young. They have striven in every way, not only to manage the camp economically, but to do their part towards giving the boys a pleasant and profitable visit, and they have succeeded admirably. Lastly, with regard to the true aim of the camp, i.e., to be of positive and lasting benefit to all who visit it, here also we can trace a steady progress as the years have passed. One important step has been the gradual determination of the type of boys we can help most.

We can select them with more discernment, and treat them more wisely. Every year we have fewer perfectly unimpressionable "toughs,' and over impressionable spoiled children, two classes with which we vainly experimented during our early experience. This kind of progress is less easy to describe and explain than the improvements in buildings, but those who have kept in touch with the camp through its eight years of existence know that its work has broadened and grown steadily more effective. S. V. S.

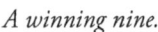
A winning nine.

The Purpose Of The Camp

The regeneration of the world is a knotty problem which has vexed mankind and has given rise to many philosophies. Modern experience, the practical philosophy of the day, seems to teach that there is no short-cut to salvation and that the raising of mankind is a slow and tedious process which can be accomplished only by persistent work on the individual. The nursery rhyme has it that

> *"Little drops of water,*
> *Little grains of sand,*
> *Make the mighty ocean,*
> *And the pleasant land."*

and it is undoubtedly true that the ocean of reform, both political and social, will be the mass of the drops of small individual endeavor which are the characteristic sign of our modern civilization, that no work is too small or too insignificant and that the only way to accomplish great results is to do thoroughly the small work which is at our door and to awaken in the individuals with whom we come in contact a recognition of what is good and noble in life. It is extraordinary how far a single act may reach in the complexities of modern intercourse, whether for good or for evil. Perhaps the most encouraging sign of the times is the recognition of this fact as shown by the willingness of men to take part in the various agencies which are working, each within a limited sphere, to raise the standard of life of the uneducated and of the vicious.

A democracy which restricts equality to political rights or to equality of opportunity is a step forward, but fails very short of the ideal.

The crews practicing.

I take it that in a true democracy there must be equality of intercourse, and equality of intercourse can come only from real sympathy and a fellowship with character wherever found. As life grows more complicated with the advance of material wealth and the formation of social classes, we seem in a fair way to lose the equality of intercourse which was the boast of our early days. We need to come in contact on terms of equality with the large masses of our countrymen who have had none of the advantages we have had showered on us, and to measure ourselves with them to see whether our opportunities have really modified human nature or have simply given us superficial advantages which might be attained by the lowest under certain conditions. I think that the most carefully nurtured and the best bred, when they come into intimate contact with the vicious and the neglected, will find in themselves possibilities which might have degraded them to the level of these unfortunates, and will find in the lowest the possibilities of generosity and of devotion which, under more favorable circumstances, might have raised those who seemed doomed to poverty and vice to a noble and useful life. It is because Groton School was conscious of these two facts—that every man has work to do for humanity and that in order to be democratic one must learn to know one's fellows—that the camp was undertaken. We are one of the numberless agencies working, in a small way, to improve the condition of the poor. We are trying to do what the Social Settlements, the Boys' Clubs, the Country Weeks, and such like are doing, adding our drop to the ocean. We take a number of boys for a short time let them live a clean, healthy, out-of-door life, in touch with nature, in beautiful surroundings, and in the companionship of men and boys who are trying to live rightly and highly. It is an infinitesimal effort and cannot have much of a direct effect on the great problem, but the indirect possibilities are enormous for only imagine what might be accomplished by the Groton boys when they grow to be men if they carry on the work of which they have had a taste as boys. And this is what is to my mind the great use and potential power of place like our school camp. Our boys come from well-to do, often from luxurious homes; they have been carefully guarded from suffering and from the sight of suffering; their knowledge of mankind has been restricted to a small and prosperous circle; and they naturally grow to think that they somehow differ radically from the poor boys they meet in the street. But let these same Groton boys live for a week or two in constant companionship with ragged street urchins, working with them, playing with them, and they will soon discover that the feeling, the tastes, and even the manners of these little bootblacks are not so very different from their own.

They are taught a lesson in equality which may materially modify their conception of the inborn superiority of the educated and refined. We get our boys from various sources—from boys' clubs, from church choirs, from charity bureaus, sometimes from reform schools—and always try to get the poorest and the neediest. We live with them on the freest terms for a couple of weeks, taking our share in their work and in their play. The effect on them is of course not far-reaching. They catch a glimpse of the happier side of life; they see the hills and the waters; they are surrounded by kindliness and decency; and they go back to their narrow lives. It is but a drop in the ocean. But the effect on us is very great. We have taken a hand in the work of social up-lifting, we have broadened our sympathies and we have begun to enter into our birthright of democratic living. The governing body of the camp is a Groton master, a permanent resident, who is often a master or a graduate of Groton, and some six or seven graduates and older boys who come for a week or a fortnight. During this time we are occupied in keeping our charges busy and happy. It is a valuable lesson in philanthropy and Groton parents must realize what an opportunity their boys have to learn, under favorable circumstances, the first steps in the road of higher service. Such a charity is of necessity dependent on the generosity of its friends and we ask those who are interested in Groton School to help us maintain a work which we believe has justified the expense of its maintenance.

Cheerful Types

The camp day regularly begins with the sounding of the first horn. Sometimes there is a member of the faculty who has piscatorial pretensions, which lead, or rather mislead, him to begin the day at some unknown early hour. He then goes out in the dark and rows to some place where, according to obscure legends, fish have been known to bite, and three or four hours later while the camp is at breakfast he returns with a fine string of stories of the fine bass that he would have caught if his lines or his hooks or his bait had been different or if the ripple on the water had rippled in a different way.

On the wharf

There is also a possible stirring of maternal life which the dormitory "master" may experience. A camp law requires silence in the dormitory until the first horn is heard. But when the morning is light and warm, and the birds and squirrels are chattering in the trees, there are often wakeful youngsters who have an irrepressible impulse to emit various calls and cries. This often makes a bad three-quarters of an hour for the "facticle" who is responsible for peace in the dormitory. When the horn finally blares out from the cook's headquarters, it is answered by a general whoop, and in a moment the camp is alive with swarming nudities hurrying down to the lake for the morning dip. This early plunge in the water is required of all and is usually taken as a delightful privilege. Occasionally, however, there is sonic youth with a hydrophobic disinclination to it, and such aversions have to be overcome by force. The faculty meanwhile perform their ablutions in the delightful "bath-tub" in the rear of the tents, which was last year rendered especially commodious and convenient by the elaborate constructions carried out by V. R. L. and G. H., structures which I fear have not survived the movement and pressure of the winter ice floes. The breakfast hour is seven o'clock, though slight variations owing to the way the kitchen fire burns or to the elaborateness of the menu may be expected. Breakfast consists of oatmeal or mush, stew or fish. warm rolls or Johnnycake and plenty of milk and butter. Alter breakfast and before leaving the tables, prayers are said. The next two or three hours are devoted to "morning work." This part of the day's programme is not altogether popular with the boys. The faculty usually engage in it with enthusiasm. In particular those who have charge of the wood-cutting find pleasant exhilaration in the vigorous exercise under the fragrant forest, where they can work themselves into sympathy with Gladstone, Abraham Lincoln, and other mighty wielders of the axe.

By force of example and by judicious and persistent stimulus the young lads can be led to a fairly hearty performance of their part in the work. Considerable wisdom is needed to draw nicely the line between leading and pushing. The chief of the dormitory squad must not be too dainty to grasp himself the mop and the scrub cloth, he must not shrink from handling with his own hand the stuffy blankets. But if he goes too far in his self-sacrificing zeal he will find the kids quite ready to let him do all the work, while they loaf, or scrap, or slip away to some congenial amusement.

After the morning swim

The next event in the order of the day is swimming, and there is no mistaking the high favor which is felt toward it, coming as it does after the fatigues and trials of morning work. There are always some good swimmers, and also some who cannot swim at all. These latter generally acquire the art, or at least make a beginning of it, during their two weeks' stay in camp. A half hour is the traditional limit for this exercise, but it may sometimes be stretched without detriment to forty minutes. Twelve o'clock is the usual hour for dinner, where hearty appetites and great capacity for the absorption of food are manifested. After dinner, the dormitory squad finish their labors by taking in the blankets which have been airing during the morning. These are neatly folded and laid upon the beds.

The afternoon is given up to some organized form of amusement. It may be a trip to the shore for base-ball or for berries, or a party goes to Holderness prepared for an assault on the sellers of candy and soda water. Sometimes a long row around the lake, exploring the various caves and islands, and observing the different camps and cottages, fills an afternoon pleasantly. Sometimes an infatuated fisherman takes a select party off in pursuit of his favorite delusion. An ascent of Rattlesnake Mountain or of Red Hill is another diversion of great interest, though it requires considerable effort to carry it out harmoniously. One of the pleasantest days is the one which is given up to a picnic. On this day, morning work is slightly abridged. Swimming is deferred until the picnic grounds, or some sandy beach on the way thither, are reached. The party all embark in the boats before dinner, carrying the cook and his kettles and the needful cups and dishes. A landing is made at some charming spot, after a voyage of one or two hours. Then a feast of soup or stew, gingerbread and other dainties is devoured with great relish, as the party sits or reclines upon the grass.

A game of ball or some other form of sport, or a tramp to explore some new place in the forest, or an ascent of some hill makes the hours of the day go by rapidly. The return to camp is made by five or six o'clock. There, another swim is taken and then supper follows. Reading and various house games occupy many after supper. Then, when the kitchen crew have finished their labors, the various boat crews go out for practice, and others go in the large boats to watch them, so that the whole camp is often afloat for an hour or more in the sunset time. At eight o'clock all gather in the dining-room for evening prayer. Here, one or two hymns are sung, and then all the boys go to bed.

The later hours of evening are employed by the faculty in various ways. Some, who have social inclinations, pay visits to their friends at other camps. Some join in a game of cards in the dining-room, and regale themselves with cookies or other provisions which the munificence of the cook sets forth. Sometimes, when the moonlight is fine, they go out in boats for a quiet drift on the lake, and this forms a most blissful ending to a day in camp.

Groton School camp kitchen and cook.

Squam Steam Boat leaving the camp.

Chapter 5

GROTON SCHOOL CAMP HISTORY (2)

A REPRINT FROM THE 1942 GROTONIAN

BY

REV. ENDICOTT PEABODY

&

ACOSTA NICHOLS

Groton School staff from the highest point on Mayhew Island—the new home for the Camp. Reverend Endicott Peabody on far right. c.1920

The Groton School Camp

BY ENDICOTT PEABODY, AND ACOSTA NICHOLS, Jr. '30, *Manager of the Camp*
(Reprinted from the 1942 Groton School Quarterly)

THE SCHOOL CAMP WAS THE OUTCOME OF A DESIRE on the part of the members of the Missionary Society to extend our field of usefulness. During the first two years, the School had held service in a room in the High School building for such people as cared especially for our prayer book worship. We had done some things for our neighbors, and later we had started in some of the towns in our vicinity, mission stations, which developed into the Parish of St. Andrew's in Ayer and Groton. In looking about our cities, we discovered that nothing was being done for the boys who, on account of limited resources, were unable to leave their homes and enjoy for a brief period a vacation in the hottest season of the year.

We had heard something of the practice of English Public Schools[1] which were in the habit of taking several hundred boys to the seashore, keeping them in tents, looking after them, and giving them an outing of two or three weeks in the summer.

It seemed to us worthwhile to establish a permanent site for a summer camp and there to entertain through the season a fairly large number of boys, taking them a fortnight each in smaller groups with a view to getting into closer relationship with the individuals. The plan was adopted enthusiastically and we began to look about for the best possible site for our new project. A perfect spot was soon discovered in New Hampshire in the midst of a beautiful, mountainous country, and on one of the loveliest of lakes we purchased the ground for our enterprise. We selected an island, not only for its outstanding attraction, but also with a view to the safekeeping of the boys. This plan seemed to be justified shortly after our start—one of the youngsters, attacked by nostalgia, demanded a passage to his home. During all these years, he said, Mother had worked for him and now he wanted to do some work for her. He was assured that this outing would make him more useful for Mother. This suggestion and the island keep restrained him from a desertion which would have been possible, indeed, probable, if we had been living on the mainland. As it was, he cheered up in a few hours and seemed to enjoy his outing thoroughly.

The island having been selected, subscriptions came in promptly as they always will when one has a scheme which promises to be of service to the community. We purchased the place, and on it we erected a dormitory, kitchen and playroom, and tents for the "facticles" (as our

---

[1]*Describes an English influence for the idea of Groton School Camp. Endicott Peabody was schooled in England and was influenced by some of their customs.*

Tea time. Inspecting new camp construction on Mayhew Island. Approx 1920. (Rev. Peabody at right.)

Swedish cook called the masters and boys who composed the staff).

Incidentally, the idea of a summer camp had just been devised by one Ernest Balch who should be regarded as a great philanthropist. This first camp, partly, no doubt, a financial venture, but also an attempt to supply an opportunity for a wholesome summer life for boys, was followed by a second camp of similar nature, again on Lake Asquam.

Ours was the first camp which enabled what is sometimes called the "underprivileged boy" to enjoy this sort of outdoor life equally with the more fortunate. Both kinds of camps have spread throughout the country. There are thousands of summer camps for boys, and a great number of schools have established permanent camps at which their students find pleasure in assisting.

This camp of ours began its life on Groton Island in Lake Asquam in July 1893. It commended itself to all boys, with few exceptions, who were invited to enjoy their outing with us. There was an abundance of activities for each day, beginning with assisting Andrew in the kitchen where he prepared most acceptable nourishment and maintained order with the assistance of his paddle which stood by the door. Then came careful policing of the camp, followed by baseball, the ground for which was cleared by succeeding groups of foresters; swimming, carefully supervised by a "facticle" who from time to time helped to rescue some inexperienced city boy who thought that the water was there to support him without effort on his part; rowing about the lake; fishing, not always synonymous with catching fish; and opportunities for good fellow-ship in which all took a ready part.

From the beginning, there were encouraging results. The health of our visitors was indicated by the increase of weight of each individual. Abundant evidence of the appreciation of life at camp has been given through all the succeeding years. It has not been uncommon for us to meet men of middle age who speak of the summer holidays at Asquam as one of the happiest of their boyhood memories. Last spring, I met in far-off Tucson a man who described with delight his recollection of life at the Camp. He had been there in the early part of the century, but it was all fresh in his mind, and when I began the camp cheer of 1915 he finished it with enthusiasm and accuracy.

There was indeed a general tendency for those who stayed with us and those who worked at the camp to be drawn closely together, and our boys became aware that there was as much variety in the personality of the boys from the cities as is found in the boarding schools to which they belonged. There was a further advantage to our representatives not only in the consciousness that they were learning a great deal, but also in the feeling of satisfaction that part of their vacation was devoted to others rather than themselves.

So we began and so we continued for many happy years. During that time there was a general approval of the camp. As the charms of the lake and mountains became better known, there drifted into the neighbourhood people who established country houses, the peace of which seemed to them disturbed by boys somewhat noisier than they cared to endure, and it became increasingly evident that a change of venue would be welcomed by them. No doubt they thought it would be to the advantage of our camp and its supporters. Accordingly, we accepted the offer of one of our opulent neighbors, abandoned the place in which we had spent many delightful years, and, crossing the mountains, transferred our summer abode to Newfound Lake where the precious traditions of our first summer home are carried on.

Mail Delivery by Steamer

Chapter 6

GROTON SCHOOL CAMP HISTORY

MISC. NEWS ARTICLES, LETTERS AND RECORDS

MY NEIGHBOR

A Monthly Journal of the Episcopal City Mission.

*But he, willing to justify himself, said unto Jesus,
And who is my neighbour?*

VOL. III.   BOSTON: SEPTEMBER, 1894.   No. 11.

The Groton School Camp.

An account was given a year ago, in MY NEIGHBOUR, of the summer camp instituted then at Holderness, N. H.

As the experiment was successful, it has been repeated this summer on a somewhat larger scale.

It is really a missionary work, whereby the scholars and masters of the Groton School undertake to share some of their privileges of recreation and change of scene with their poorer brethren.

Willoughby Island, lying in a picturesque cove on the northwest side of Squam Lake, has been purchased by members of the Groton School, and dormitories, a dining-room and kitchen, and other buildings, have been built near its eastern shore.

To this beautiful spot about one hundred and twenty-five poor city boys have been invited this summer, each for a fortnight's stay. A fresh installment of ten or fifteen boys arrives every Tuesday, and on the same day as many depart. Most of them are from Boston, though twenty boys come from New York.

It seems that some wealthy New York friends of the Groton School arranged a concert in behalf of this summer camp, and netted the remarkable sum of three thousand dollars. It seemed only fair, therefore, that a few boys, at least, from New York should be included in the list of invited guests.

The twenty-five lively, undisciplined boys are under the care of a "Faculty," as they are called, composed of six of the masters or older boys of the Groton School, each staying several weeks. The men who have successively been in charge of the camp, this summer, have been:— Messrs. Endicott Peabody; S. W. Sturgis, Griswold, Ayrault and Gardner, Grafton Cushing and W. R. Sturgis.

The rule in all the boys' camps, of which there are four or five on Squam Lake, is that every boy, rich or poor, shall have some two hours' real work to do after breakfast. The Groton Camp follows this excellent example, and, for two hours or more, little squads will be seen busily employed, some sawing wood for

My Neighbor

the fires, making beds, sweeping or scrubbing floors, clearing up the camp, making paths or roads, cleaning out the boats, filling lamps, helping Andrew (the cook), or doing other tasks.

Play is all the sweeter after a moderate amount of duty. The sports of the day are bathing, boating, fishing, base ball, excursions to the mountains near by, picking berries, and various athletic sports.

The Camp boys have been greatly elated because, in two formal base-ball matches with the boys of another camp on the lake, they were in both cases the victors.

When Sunday comes, the entire camp row three and a half miles, in several boats, to the little Episcopal Church on Shepard Hill—St. Peter's in the Mount—and attend the morning service. As many of the boys are members of our mission choirs, their voices are a most welcome help in the singing. The presence, too, of so large a company of boys and young men, is of itself very interesting, both to the congregation and the clergyman.

These one hundred boys, many of them from demoralizing surroundings, not only have a healthful and happy visit in one of the most picturesque spots in the land, with every accompaniment which ministers to innocent enjoyment, but they are sure, from the manly, earnest spirit of the Camp, and the personal influence of the young men in charge, to get some new impressions of an ideal Christian manhood.

The majority of these boys are from the churches of the Episcopal City Mission, and we count it a pleasure to put them in the way of so rich and delightful an experience.

Frederick B. Allen

Article from "My Neighbor",

A Monthly Journal of the Episcopal City Mission, Boston September 1894.

May 26. Called to see a most wretched family. The mother's face is so disfigured by a burn she received when a chid that she is something frightful to see. Her husband is a drunkard, and her father who is quite an old man, came in drunk while I was there. He told me that he did not believe there was any hereafter. I read them a chapter. They were attentive and quiet while I was there.

June 2. Called to see the wretched K. family. Did not see the mother. I think she had hidden away in some place. The son was in another room in bed, drunk, so his sister told me. She showed me where he had kicked her black and blue, while she was trying to save her mother from his blows. There was hardly a thing in the room that was not broken. The panels of the door were out, with an old piece of carpet nailed over them.

June 5. Called to see Mrs. P. She told me a heart-rending story of her misery with a drunken husband. Yesterday he stood over his little girl with a poker, and had the mother not come between, murder might have heen comitted. He has said several times that he would kill his wife. She is afraid to complain, for he has told her he surely would kill her if she did. June 12. Had a very distressitig case to deal with today. Mrs. D. sent for me to come and see her. I found a sad state of things. Her drunken husband had gone off and left her with four children—the oldest seven years and the youngest three weeks old. She had only provisions for three days, was in debt, and her furniture was not paid for.* She said she would like to take her baby to her sister in Newfoundland, who would take it for her own. If I could get the other children placed in a "Home" for a few months she would return and work for the children. The matron of the "Gwynne Home" will take them in a week or so. Have given her a little aid, and will speak to the Provident Association about her.

* For the past three years her husband has been drinking badly, earning about $18.00 a week as a jeweller and giving her but seven. Lately on account of his habits he has been out of work.

The Missionary Society

Executive Committee, 1923-1924

Mr. S. W. Sturgis..............................President
E. C. Childs, '24............................Vice-President
J. W. G. Tenney, '24..........................Secretary
H. Southworth, '25............................Treasurer

E. Field, '24   J. Lawrence, Jr., '25

MEMBERS

The Fifth Form   The Faculty   The Sixth Form

CAMP COMMITTEE

Chairman   *Treasurer*
Mr. F. P. Nash, Jr., '16   E. C. Childs, '24

C. T. Bingham, '24   O. Driggs, '24   J. W. G. Tenney, '24

CHRISTMAS TREE COMMITTEE

Chairman
E. C. Childs, '24

W. Maynard, '24   G. A. Sanderson, Jr., '24   J. Lawrence, Jr., '25

MISSIONARIES

To Forge Village
E. C. Childs, '24   W. Maynard, '24

To Shirley
H. E. Heard, '24   J. W. G. Tenney, '24

Permanent Resident of the School Camp
Summer of 1924
Arthur Milliken, '22

127

The Missionary Society

The Groton School Missionary Society is no close corporation. For a short period in its early history membership was elective, but for many years now it has been open to all masters, and boys of the fifth and sixth forms. Its aim is two-fold; to broaden the necessarily limited outlook of our small community, and to enable the older boys to do some sort of work for others.

The first aim is furthered by visits and addresses from missionaries and workers in different forms of social service. In following the second aim we have tried to be of use to the community around us. We have helped to establish Sunday-schools, and later on, mission-centres, in Ayer, East Shirley and Forge Village. Some years a series of services was arranged in outlying district schoolhouses. We have run a circulating library of magazines, helped in the work of neighboring boy-scout units, raised money for all sorts of worthy causes, and in general tried to be of some service outside our own school boundaries.

But far and away the most important activity of the Missionary Society has been the Fresh-air Camp in New Hampshire; which during the past thirty-one years has annually given a healthy summer outing to about 170 little guests from the city, and a valuable experience to 40 or 50 of our own graduates and boys. The Camp was opened in the Summer of 1893 and

SWIMMING TIME AT THE SCHOOL CAMP

had all the interest of a new experiment (in such work). We had no experience and no other camps of this sort to study as models. But, from the moment when the Rector suggested the idea, the School took it up eagerly. Masters, graduates (among whom Dick Wheatland, '91; Bill Patten, '91; Phil Smith, '95, and Julian Gerard, '94, were especially zealous), parents and boys backed up the new venture; and from the very first year the Camp has unquestionably justified the necessary expenditure of time, money and effort.

Our first site was on a small island in Lake Asquam, where we gradually developed an attractive and complete equipment; and where for twenty-eight years we enjoyed the beautiful view of Red Hill across the lake, and the varied charms of High Haith, the Rattlesnakes, Mt. Livermore and Squaw Cove. It was indeed a region where "every prospect pleased, and only man was" too numerous. Various features incidental to the growing popularity of Asquam, and the difficulty of obtaining milk and other local supplies for our hungry outfit, induced us four years ago to sell Groton Island and move elsewhere. It was a big move, managed most successfully by the able and untiring zeal of Barclay Farr '08, with the generous help of Mr. J. Randolph Coolidge, Jr., who designed and super-

GROTON SCHOOL YEAR BOOK

intended the building of the new camp. We are now reëstablished most satisfactorily on a 50-acre island in New Found Lake, N. H.

So many Grotonians have shared in the actual running of the Camp that it seems hardly necessary in such a book as this to give many details of its life and methods. The Faculty consists of the "P. R.," who is the responsible permanent resident, and a constantly changing group of masters, graduates and older boys from Groton. There are also two paid assistants, who remain all summer and preside over the important kitchen department. Financially the Camp is largely dependent on subscriptions from interested friends. Transportation and provisions come high; and, though the Stillman endowment fund yields us $1,000 a year, we have to raise an additional $2,500 to cover expenses.

It has been stated as the aim of Groton Camp that "it may prove a lasting benefit to all who visit it." We have been singularly fortunate in freedom from illness and accident, the high purpose of the early years has been kept steadily in view, and we may safely feel that practically all, both helpers and guests, have definitely profited by their camp experience.—S. W. STURGIS.

THE SHACKS

Former Permanent Residents of the School Camp

1893	T. P. Thurston
1894	G. Z. Gray, '91
1895	E. H. Newbegin
1896	E. F. Chauncey, '92
1897	T. P. Thurston
1898	E. H. Newbegin
1899	G. P. Campbell
1900	Fred Young
1901	Fred Young
1902	T. P. Thurston
1903	M. H. Birckhead, '98
1904	M. H. Birckhead, '98
1905	M. W. Rice
1906	J. D. Nichols, '02
1907	H. Gray, '04, and G. Biddle, '04
1908	J. T. Addison, '05
1909	G. A. Richardson, '06
1910	B. H. Farr, '08
1911	B. H. Farr, '08
1912	R. W. Baker, '09, and D. S. Hawkins, '08
1913	H. M. Atkinson, '11
1914	W. Willcox, '13
1915	D. S. Hawkins, '98
1916	Ralph E. Bailey
1917	Closed on account of the War
1918	Closed on account of the War
1919	C. J. Mason, '18
1920	F. P. Nash, '16
1921	Louis Dejonge, '19
1922	S. Bradford, '20
1923	F. D. Ashburn, '21

129

Letter From Camp (1894)

DEAR MOTHER, I HOPE YOU ARE WELL. It is a 150 miles from Boston to hear . I first took the steam car and when we got out—we got into a hay cart and drove to a hotel and got our dinner and then road 7 miles in the same team and then we took 3 boats and road to hear, and when we got here there was to houses, the 1 to sleep in the other to eat in and it is more than fine out here. We all get to our table and stand up and then the man says a grace and then we neele down and said a prayer all together and then he says three more and then we eat and afterwards we have prayers out doors and in the morning we work till half past ten and then we in swimming and we take the three boats and where ever we go , there is a man with us. There is a cook and just now there is only 9 boys. In the afternoon we go fishing and I tell you we are in it when we were coming here we were hollering, shouting, singing and dancing in the hay cart and it was go fast all the time and when we got to an hill we would all get out and be picking flowers on the way. We slick our own beds and there are 4 boys to wash and wipe the dishes and 3 to make the beds and there are too boys to go and milk the cows and two different boys go every morning. There is lots and lots more things I would like to tell you about but there is so much fun out here that I want to be having some. I am just scribbling this over for I want to have some fun. I only wish we could live out here so goodbye.—love to all.

Yours truly-

Letter from Camp (1894)

DEAR MOTHER,—PLEASE GIVE SISTER—and all some kisses for me. I hope you are well. We all went to church Sunday and Mr. Peabody was our minister that is the head one of us. There is ten more Boys coming here tomorrow. I was upon a high mountain yesterday and to-day I am on an island and when I want to go for the male I have to row over in a boat. I am having a very—very nice time out here. Over at the church is out in the air and it is all sand and a great big cross at the entrance and at the end. There is a horn blows here at 8 o'clock and that means for all of us to get into the bed rooms and get undressed and sit on the end of our beds and at a quarter past 8 Mr. Peabody reads a long prayer and then we get down on our knees and say "Our Father" and then he says the three last prayers that our minister says at the end of the morning and evening prayers and then the horn blows for all to get into their beds—men and all of us and the men have to obey what Mr. Peabody says. The horn blows in the morning at half past 6 and then we have breakfast at 7 and then we make the beds and then we go to work taking brush and putting it in the scow. We are making two tents for the other Boys. And you know Mr. Allen that comes to our church and preaches—that is the minister—well he was here today and he knew us three boys from church. And he he took 4 different pictures of all of us. After we work till half past 10 and then we go fishing until a 11 o'clock and then we go in swimming. I can swim now. I think that is all. Goodbye. Will you please send me some stamps.

Your loving son -

The Grotonian October 1893

THE MEMBERS OF THE FIRST GROTON SCHOOL CAMP FACULTY met together at Ashland, N. H., on July 3rd, two days before the formal opening of the Camp, for the purpose of getting together supplies, and preparing to receive the first set of boys on July 5th. After purchasing the necessary things at Ashland, and making arrangements for the summer supplies; the faculty, and also the cook who joined the party here, drove seven miles towards the western end of Lake Asquam, where the camp was to be established. On arriving at the Island, which contained about three acres of thick woods, the long sleeping shanty was found to be completed, as was also the dining-room and the kitchen adjoining. None of the dishes had arrived, and the stove could not be set up that night; so the faculty had to be content with eating bread and butter and sardines off wooden boards.

The next day, the morning was spent in completing arrangements with the farmers about supplying milk, eggs, etc., and in putting in order whatever supplies had come. In the afternoon the three boats arrived, in which, afterwards under the charge of one of the faculty, the youngsters rowed many an exciting race.

It was thought advisable to start the camp with a small number. So on July 5th, one of the faculty came, bringing with him seven small urchins. Yet, notwithstanding their diminutive size, the yells of delight, which they emitted at the sight of every strange object, could be heard for several minutes before the hay-rick, in which they were being transported, came into sight

The work done in these first two weeks was mostly directed toward cleaning away the thick woods in the immediate vicinity of the buildings, and in opening up a vista towards the mountains at the upper end of the lake. While this was progressing, some of the faculty were occupied in making several necessary additions to the buildings, and building a large tent platform, with a piazza in front. One of the highest trees on the island was utilized as a flag-pole, but even this was found to be too low; and later in the summer was replaced by a pole given by a friend of the Camp.

In this way the days, intermingled with many swims, boat-races, walks, and games of baseball, passed too quickly by, and the first faculty soon found that it was time for them to leave, and give place to their successors.

The Camp, during the second two weeks of the summer holidays, was as pleasant, I am sure, as it was at any other time. It had got into very good running order, and the poor boys certainly felt quite at home, so much so, that when we arrived, they treated us as if we were to be their guests. They were, however, a very good set of fellows, obliging and for the most part, willing to work. There were some, of course, who were naturally lazy, and it was not until these caught the spirit of the Camp that they could be prevailed on to do any work.

Every morning there was great activity in Camp from eight till eleven o'clock, when the boys were divided into squads to clean the boats, wash the dishes, make the beds, and clear away the rubbish from about the buildings. They were all very smart and we had little difficulty in teaching them their various kinds of work. One boy stayed in the same squad only for three or four days; so that at the end of two weeks he had acquired a certain degree of efficiency in each branch of the work. At eleven o'clock there was a general rush for the boats which took the boys, under the charge of several members of the faculty, to Sandy beach for Swimming. The boys showed such complete absence of timidity in the water, that the task of teaching them to swim was an easy one. They were not allowed to stay in the water very long, so that the bath had a refreshing and not an enervating effect on them. We were all ready for dinner at half past twelve, and did justice to the excellent meal which Andrew, our cook, had ready for us. It consisted of soup, meat, two or three vegetables and a pudding. A quiet half hour generally followed dinner, and at half-past two we began our afternoon's amusement. Sometimes we went to the mainland where a large field, set aside for our use, enabled us to have a good game of ball. Occasionally we took the boys to gather blueberries. This they enjoyed immensely and spent several hours, picking in perfect content. We sometimes also spent the afternoon in climbing some high mountain, from whose summit we could get a fine view. After a long tramp of this kind, the boys felt pretty tired and were often unwilling to indulge in our after-supper sport—rowing races, Usually, however, this was not the case and the two crews were eager for a race, which they rowed over a course in front of the camp. At eight o'clock, prayers were read and the boys then went to the dormitory to go to bed. The faculty spent the rest of the evening in playing games. At an early hour we went to our tents and slept soundly until the horn awoke us at half-past six on the following morning.

The nine boys, who were taken in charge at the Lowell depot in Boston on August 22 were to be in camp for the last two weeks of the season. The journey to Ashland and the drive over to the camp were attended by no special incidents. In due time Sleeper's landing was reached where the boys were meet by Mr. Thurston and Converse, and soon after they were on the lovely Camp ground where they met Mr. Thayer, the master in charge and W. H. Hare, the other member of the faculty. Mr. Thayer turned over the camp to his successor, who then took up the interesting and agreeable employment of superintending it for the next two weeks. On Thursday the 24th Wheatland arrived and entered upon duty as a member of the faculty. The weather was fair for the most part A few storms of rain and wind had an autumnal chill which made one wish for a camp fire. On the 29th Hare, who had served on the faculty for two weeks, left, taking back to Boston the boys whose time was out. On the same day Alsop arrived with ten new boys to complete the quota for the last week. Converse remained until Sept 1st, when he and Wheatland departed for Maine.

This is not the place to record all the daily incidents which gave zest and interest to the camp life. A notable event was an evening spent at Chocorua camp to which the Groton School camp was invited by Dr. and Mrs. Huntington, who with some young ladies, their guests, entertained the boys with games and fed them lavishly with ice cream and cake. On the way home little Leonard Taylor (surnamed "Peesar"), who had done wonders in the comsumption of ice cream, fell fast asleep in the stern of the boat.

A note of sadness was struck amid the general joyousness, when one afternoon a dispatch arrived announcing the death of the mother of two of the boys. Mr. Thurston took them off at once to Ashland, and succeeded in getting them aboard an express train for Boston.

In the book of the camp chronicles it is written how Hare and Converse sat on a rail fence to gaze at the moon, and how the treacherous rail broke and "deposited them in a cavity" and in the water six or eight feet below; how Alsop disciplined Geo. Read, the prizefighter's brother; how Patten had numberless "scraps's with Andrew; how Wheatland fired numerous shots with his rifle at a supposed loon which later proved to be a floating shoe; and how various ball-games, boat races and mountain parties occurred. The camp received numerous visits, among which may be mentioned those of Rev. Mr. Allen and the ladies of his family, and Mr. Balsh, the founder of Camp Chocorua, who made many interesting suggestions regarding camp matters.

On Saturday, Sept. 2nd, Mr. Sturgis and his brother Mr. Ned Sturgis arrived, the former coming up to superintend the closing of the camp and the storage of the goods. On Sept. 5th the tents were taken down, the boys and the faculty formed a procession about the camp, saluting each building with the Camp cheer, and singing "Rally round the flag," and "My country 'tis of thee" beneath the flag-staff. Then they bade adieu to the island, leaving Mr. Sturgis and Mr. Thurston, who gave two days of hard labor to the final disposition of the Camp property. The movable goods were all transported to Camp Chocorua, and the buildings on the island were fastened up to secure them against tramps and squirrels—and so the campaign was over.

Our Summer Camp was certainly the greatest success and we earnestly hope that our friends may help us with contributions to repeat next summer what has this year given two weeks of pleasure to each of nearly two hundred boys.

Picnic on the mainland

From The
New York Herald—Sunday March 18, 1894

THERE IS IN PREPARATION, under the skilful guidance of Mrs. Gerard and Mrs. Wilmerding, a splendid concert to be given early next month in aid of the Summer Camp for Poor Boys, which was so successfully organized by the Rev. Endicott Peabody, of the famous Groton School, a year ago. By the results of a concert given in New York last April two hundred poor boys from this city and Boston had during last summer all the benefits of the Camp.

This Camp is on the borders of Lake Asquam, in New Hampshire and there boys are taken from squalid and miserable homes in the slums of great cities. They have a certain amount of intellectual instruction and are also taught manly sports, rowing, swimming and sailing, and above all they are associated with young gentlemen and influences are brought to bear upon them which must be felt all through their lives, and which they carry back to their own homes to spread among their families and companions.

The young gentlemen in charge of the Camp under the direction of Mr. Peabody belong to families of greatest prominence in New York and Boston, and they give up a part of their own summer holiday, leaving the pleasures of Newport or Bar Harbor to go and live at the Camp and lend themselves to the good work.

Through the efforts of Mrs. Gerard and Mrs. Wilmerding, Mme. Melba. Signor Ancona, Henri Marteau and other artists have generously offered their services The concert will take place some afternoon between April 17 and 25 in the large ballroom at Sherry's.

Some of the people who will aid in making the concert a financial success are Mrs. J. Pierpont Morgan, Mrs. Buchanan Winthrop, Mrs. Charles T. Barney Miss May Callender, Miss Caroline Deforest. Mrs. William D. Sloane, Mrs. Edward R. Bell, Mrs. James A. Burden, Mrs. Walter Cutting, Mrs. William H. Dr. Per, Miss Clementine Furniss, Mrs. Morgan Dix, Mrs. Alfred L. Edwards, Mrs. Townsend Burden, Mrs. Fulton Cutting, Mrs. S. B. Chittenden, Mrs. William P. Jaffray, Mrs. Adrian Iselin. Jr., Mrs. Theodore A. Havemeyer, Mrs. John Jay, Mrs. Richard Irvin, Mrs. Paran Stevens, Mrs. Adolf Ladenburg. Mrs. John W. Miaturu. William E. Rogers, Mrs. William Post Mrs. Anson Phelps Stokes, Mrs. Woodbury G. Langdon, Mrs. Chester Griswold, Mrs. William Bayard Cutting, Mrs. Brayton Ives, Mrs. James H. Benedict, Mrs. Alexander S. Webb, Mrs. W. Watts Sherman, Mrs. J. Hampden, Robb, Mrs. William D. Morgan, Mrs. William, Kingslaud, Mrs. Henry G. Marquand, Mrs. J. Frederic Kernochan, Mrs. William J, Mrs. William W. Hoppin, Mrs. Abram S. Hewitt, Mrs. Clews, Mrs. Edgar S. Auchincloss, Mrs. Edmund L. Baylies, Mrs. Hitchcock. Mrs. Alexander Van Rensselaer. Mrs. Henry E. Howland, Mrs. Peter Augustus Jay, Mrs. Henry P. Rogers, Mrs. K. Sturgis, Miss Elsie De Wolfe, Mrs. Phoenix Remsen, Mr. Elbridge F. Gerry, Bishop Henry Potter, Rev. Endicott Peabody, Mr. Thomas Cushing, Mr. Perry Belmont, Mr. Richard T. Wilson, Mr. William C, Whitney, Mr. E. Randolph Robinson, Mr. Albert Morris, Bagby, Mr. John Cadwalader, Mr. William Graham, Mr. Peter Marie, Mr. George Vanderbilt and ex-Governor G. Peabody.

New York Tribune Group—1894

—By the time the boys had reached the camp they all knew the yell {camp cheer} as thoroughly and could yell it as lustily as though they had spent four years at the well-known Groton School, Instead of among the tenement-houses of New-York and Brooklyn. The farmer rested his scythe a moment, and the summer boarder changed her position slightly as the wagon drove past— NY Tribune Aug. 19, 1894

—Professor Grafton Cushing, the master in charge this week, as he welcomed the New-York boys told them that there were only two or three rules which they would be required to obey and their happyness would be based upon their obedience to them. You must not go in swimming more than three times a day, and you must not go in, the' boats without the permission of a member of the faculty, and you must not use bad language. Obey thesec rules and your stay will be a delightful one—NY Tribune Aug. 19, 1894.

Groton School Camp
By Theodore Payne Thurston 1898

THE CAMP WHICH BEARS THIS NAME had its inception in the Missionary Society of Groton School. Both the Rector of the School and the young gentlemen of the Society felt that some particularly definite work would add much to the effectiveness of the association. With this idea once in mind, the largeheartedness of the Rector, nobly seconded by the officers and members of the Society, soon perfected plans whereby a camp school be opened, to give poor city boys a summer outing.

An island in Lake Asquam, near Holderness, N. H., was selected as the spot for the camp, and arrangements were at once begun. This was in the spring of 1893. That summer: camp opened with the Rector of Groton in charge, the writer as Superintendent, and four or five young gentlemen from the School, all of whom constitute the " Faculty "—or "facticles"as the boys say. The object of the camp is primarily to give poor boys in Boston and New York at least two weeks of pleasant outdoor summer life. Their physical well being is first of all taken into account; they are taught to row, to swim; to exercise intelligently; they climb mountains; and they have abundance of pure, wholesome well cooked food. Nor is their moral nature neglected. The influence of facticles Senior member, Superintendent, and students is all on the side of decency, order, and a high moral tone. So that the object of the camp in relation to the boys is really a double one—physical first, and then spiritual. A second object is also accomplished in the bringing of more fortunate boys into such close relations with these poor children from the slums. The camp has been most admirably planned from its beginning, and has now just closed its sixth successful year. On the island have been built a commodious dormitory; a dining room, with kitchen attached, and a raised floor for the tents of the "Faculty." These buildings form a semicircle looking out over the water of the lake, which is only a few feet away. In more recent years an infirmary and a large play-house have been added, the former, fortunately, never having been put to the use for which it was built.

The boys number twenty-eight, rotating each week in squads of twenty and eight. The camp opens with twenty boys. These are taught the customs and duties of the routine life there, so that by the next Tuesday, when the eight new boys come, they all fall right into the regular routine, and so the continuity of the camp is maintained. Each boy stays two weeks, except in a few cases, when for especially meritorious conduct one may be invited to stay a third week.

On arrival each boy is furnished with a towel, soap, and a comfortable cot in the dormitory. The few rules of the camp are then explained to him, and he at once takes his place in the company. There are only two rules, and these are essential to guard against accidents: no boy may swim or enter the water except at the appointed hours; no boy may sit on or enter a boat except by permission. To the strict observance of these rules the camp owes its freedom from any accidents thus far in its history.

The routine of the camp is very simple, but quite effective. The boys are divided into squads, whose names designate the duties of each: Kitchen, Yard, Dormitory, Wood, Tents, etc. except the kitchen, which is most effectively administered by an excellent cook, the squads are presided over by several members of the "Faculty." The camp day begins nominally at seven o'clock, although for at least an hour before then many of the boys are awake and ready to arise. At seven the horn arouses every one, and there is a grand rush for the morning bath. Occasionally a timid youth must be "persuaded." or "assisted" to this necessary ablution. The assistance is quite readily given by the boys who enjoy the water. The means by which the assistance is applied is frequently a pail, or the willing arms of several boys. After two or three mornings all the boys are quite anxious to enter the water of their own accord, and so dispense with outside help. Breakfast follows at seven thirty. A short rest prepares us all for the morning's light work; the dormitory is swept and cleaned, and blankets are aired; the boots and lamps well burnished; the yard is cleaned and raked; the woodpile well stacked. Then a half hour's rest brings all the camp together again for the morning swim. This hour is one of the most enioyable of the day. There are always two or three of the "Faculty" on hand to render assistance if necessary, and give instruction when required. At twelve a hearty dinner always receives its merited attention. The afternoon is devoted to base-ball on the mainland, or athletic sports on land or water; boat racing, fishing, climbing mountains, hunting berries, rowing to Holderness, or any of those things which the fancy of the youngsters dictates. On all these occasions the young men from Groton aid materially in the successful and happy carrying out of the different plans.

At about five o'clock the dust of the day is washed off by a very short dip in the lake. Supper at six usually ends each day's routine, except when the "Kitchen crew" challenges the "camp crew" to a boat race; at which time excitement is at fever heat. At eight o'clock a hymn is sung, prayers are offered, good nights said, and the camp is silent.

On Sundays none but the necessary work is done; and all attend service at Holderness *[St. Peters on the Mount]* or at an open air chapel on an island *[Chocorura]* not far distant.

The camp has abundantly justified the hopes of its founders and has now won a deserved place among fresh air camps. The two fold object is accomplished; the boys are immensely benifited physically, while the daily morning reading from the Bible and offering of prayer, together with the closing evening hymn and prayer, bring constantly to their minds the spiritual side of their natures. The fact that it is all done in a thoroughly manly[1] way makes the teaching all the more impressive. I wish I might tell something about the funny sayings and queer customs of these boys from the slums: their peculiar language and strange ideas. They certainly present a new view of life to many of us. Their lives are by no means happy ones at home; to make them happy for at least two weeks and to impress them for all time is the great object of the camp. Nor are the boys lost sight of during the winter. A club— called "The Jefferson"— has been established by Groton graduates in Boston. This club tries to keep in touch with the boys through the winter. So, the work which began as a snmmer camp has enlarged to a winter club. The influences, physical and moral, which go out from Groton School Camp give abundant evidence of the wisdom of its founding, and commend it all who wish success to a natural method of bringing the sons of the privileged and of the unfortunate into helpful relationship.

---

[1] *Groton School subscribed to the model of "muscular Christianity". Because churches had become so associated with women and feminization in the late 19th century, Christian men began seeking changes in the nature of Christianity and Christian churches which reflected "masculine" values. In America, this early form of Muscular Christianity used sports as a conveyor of moral values, like manliness and discipline.*

(Endicott Peabody's letter to his old friend Julius W. Atwood).

Julius W. Atwood

Groton School Camp,
Holderness NH
July 17, 1893

My Dear Old Julius[1],

I HAVE THOUGHT OF YOU MUCH DURING THESE DAYS of our starting this camp on the lake where we had such a pleasant visit with Whittier in that year long ago. Whenever I row down to Shepherd Hill House I look up towards the wood giants and a feeling of the sacredness of the place comes over me—we have chosen a pleasant sight for the encampment, not the best perhaps but still good enough and convenient to the road which is a consideration when you have large numbers. We had 8 the first week. 10 more came last Tuesday. It was a little hard settling down at first but after a few days the boys discovered 1. That we intended to be their friends 2. That we would have order and so they accepted our wishes and all has gone merrily since. It is a great problem as you say, that of the relations between the rich and the poor. Our effect of this camp I hope maybe to show our boys that they can do something for others who are not as fortunate as they. . . . We shall probably invite the same boys each year, the conditions being that we get a good report of each one for the year—and this may enable us to get hold of them and to help them to help others.— E.P.

---

[1] *Whittier, the famous Quaker poet, was a friend of Julius W. Atwood.*

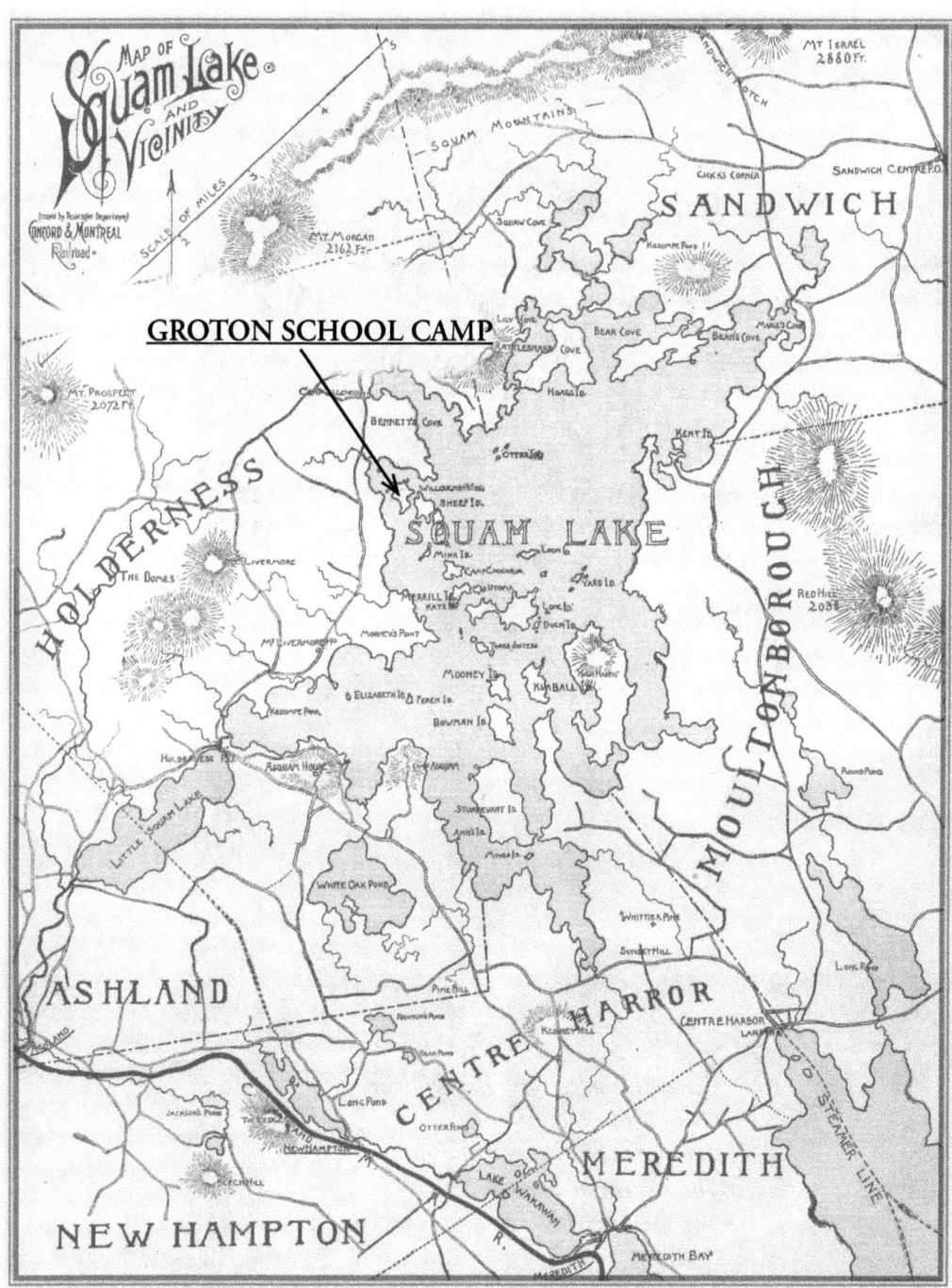

A circa 1886 map published by the Concord & Montreal Railroad..

Our toil is sweet with thankfulness,
Our burden is our boon;
The curse of earth's gray morning is
The blessing of its noon.
    —*John Greenleaf Whittier*

Part IV

GROTON SCHOOL CAMP

JOURNAL

SUMMER OF 1893

— A GLORIOUS DAY—fit day for the opening of a campaign which is full of promise — EP 1893

*—For days of drought which yet shall be
On untrod land and unsailed sea
We kneel and fill our cup of youth
At these fair fountains of Thy truth.*

*O! world all bright and brave and young
With deeds unwrought and songs unsung.
For all the strength Thy tasks will give
We greet Thee, we about to live.*[1]—

---

[1] *From the 3rd & 4th stanza of the Groton School Hymn. Written by Phillips Brooks. Music by George Peabody— great uncle of Rev. Peabody.*

Chapter 7

By
Rev. Endicott Peabody

JULY 3 - JULY 17, 1893

Reverend Endicott Peabody

Mrs. Fannie ("Frau") Peabody

T.P. Thurston

G.Z. Gray

*—The Beginning Of The History Of
Groton School Camp At
Lake Asquam[1] NH*

Monday July 3 1893

A GLORIOUS DAY–FIT DAY FOR THE OPENING of a campaign which is full of promise. There met at Boston & Lowell Station in Boston Mess. T.P. Thurston & G. Z. Gray and Rev. Endicott Peabody[2]. Took 9 am train for Ashland – (fare $4.75 for round ticket owing to failure to notify Pass. agent & so take advantage of low rate offered by Mr. Niver).

---

[1] *Now Named Squam Lake*
[2] *Reverend Endicott Peabody is the third-person author of this 1st entry; July 3 -17th.*

Boston, Concord, & Montreal Railroad

THE BOSTON, CONCORD & MONTREAL RAILROAD was chartered in 1844. Construction of the main line began in Concord in 1846. The tracks were completed to Laconia in 1848, to Ashland in 1849, and to Wells River, Vermont in 1853. The B. CM RR merged with the Concord Railroad in 1889 to form the Concord & Montreal Railroad, which was taken over by the Boston & Maine Railroad in 1895. The B, C&M RR and it's branch lines contributed greatly to the economic development of central and northern New Hampshire and to the growth of tourism in the Lakes Reqion and the White Mountains.
(Ashland Station is now a Museum.)

Campers and GS staff at train station.

Campers and Staff in front of Ashland Train Station in N.H. waiting for the hay-wagon ride to Camp.

They were joined by Mess. J.M Gerard & Philip L. Smith – thus completing the first Faculty of the Camp. A hot & not altogether comfortable journey owing to their being ensconced in a second class car which was joined at Manchester by a large Society of Hibernians[1] on a picnic. Reached Ashland 12:46 where the Cook Andrew Johnson (at once dubbed the 'Merry Andrew') was added to the company. The grocery was visited & a large portion of its stock invested in – also the tin store for the lamps and fish horns for the summoning of the Brethren in the morning and at sundry other important seasons. A beautiful dinner at Lake Asquam House renewed the spirits of the party. Proceeded—the faculty with Mr. Sleeper in the latter's 2 seated wagon— to Camp Groton. Country in its very fairest attire accorded a hearty greeting.

Lake Asquam House

Boats - not arrived
Dishes - "   "
Tools - "   "
But cots & blankets were there & we were above small inconveniences.

Dormitory and dining room completed—close by the shore—with a fine view of the lake and distant mountains. Sundry half felled trees and odd timber lying about—so much the better

---

[1] *Hibernians; an Irish Catholic Fraternal Organization.*

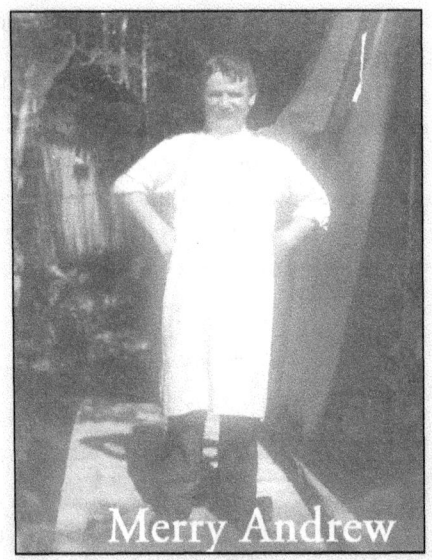
Andrew Yonson, first GS Camp cook—1893

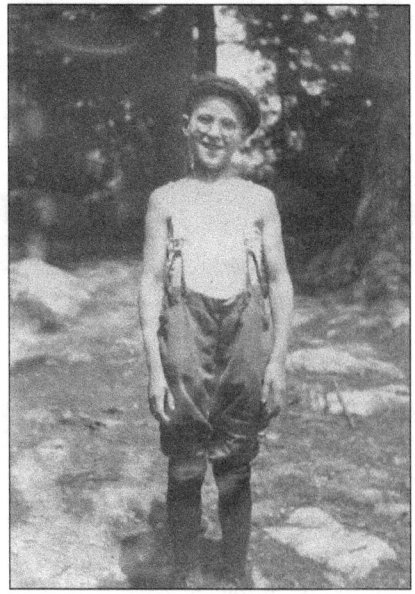
Alex, a happy camper

for it will give the youngsters work & they will take the greater interest in the place as they help to improve it.

E.P.[1] got a table into the Dorm. & estab'd himself in his nest like fashion in a corner of Dorm. The other brethren began to place cots and blankets about. Briskie and Phil Smith first to take a bath in the lake—reported it delicious. All work done that can be done. And now at 6 p.m. we are awaiting the Merry Andrew who tarries long by the way, as he has stove & all the food we feel some anxiety about him. The man who declared that mosquitoes could not be found here was singularly pachydermatous.[2] They are as large as cherries and thicker than the leaves in Vallombrosa. And with all our medicaments we brought no pennyroyal[3] Started in upon a stone dock which should be made strong & true before the end of the season. We contemplate a wooden pier running out from this and a float at the end.

At 7:15 after a swim for all us, the Merry Andrew hove in sight with provisions—a welcome visitor. Stove could not be set up. Supper served on wooden platters with wooden knives—a truly rustic scene. Food-sandwiches, bread, butter and cheese washed down with molasses & ginger and flavored with hunger—the best of all possible sauces.

Sat at table chatting for a while—instructed the M.A. in the intricacies of the gasoline stove. Prayers at 9:45 – and then turned in.

Tuesday, July 4 1893
The glorious day of Independence.
The small boy with his murderous pistol and ensnaring cannon cracker is so far distant that the night was undisturbed by the sounds of patriotic rejoicing. But the mosquitoes held high carnival. Nothing could exceed their enthusiasm.
The "Bells of Lynn" were faint in comparison. As soon as [one] was slain his whole family and all his retainers came forth to bury him and many a wake was held hard by each suffering ear.

At 4:30 mosquito netting gave a short respite to some of the Brethren. The others arose at 4:45. Julian proceeded at an early hour to Sleepers & B.B. Willoughby's where he procured eggs, milk & a few plates—so that our breakfast of ham and eggs was served in Delmonico style. After breakfast prayers. Then the party broke up. T. P. T. had departed for Boston to inquire into the causes of the long tarrying of our household chattels and to make arrangements for

[1] *Reverend Endicott Peabody*
[2] *A thick skinned mammal*
[3] *An aromatic plant of Eastern North America that yeilds an oil used as an insect repellent.*

GROTON SCHOOL CAMP — 1893 JOURNAL

Original Camp fireplace still stands.
(With imposed images of original 1893 Log Book)

the importation of the first set of boys tomorrow.

A glorious day. Bright and cool with a cheery wind. J.M.G. and E.P. proceeded, while P.L.S. and G.Z.G. were constructing a new house, to Balch's Island—(An interesting place, yet rather too citified – chapel charming) and thence to Hal Coolidge's shanties. Here a large cargo of ice was secured and moved home with some difficulty. A small steamer made her appearance at mid-day - Otherwise no human beings have been seen.

At intervals—frequent intervals—through the day P.L.S., G.Z.G. and JMG took baths. Result— —at end of day—a blind headache for P. L. S. Resolve—not to bathe so frequently—3 baths being the utmost limit and 2 baths advised. This is noted for the benefit of those who came after. The afternoon was occupied with writing of many letters on part of E.P. and manual exercise by the brethren. Tea at six. Some excellent omelettes—the Merry Andrew being an expert in this line—also noted for the benefit of posterity. At 7 P.M. a great load of freight. First and foremost, 2 large ship boats substantial & safe—and a Whitehall boat which promises to be easy to row and fast. Also numberless articles for dining room and kitchen from Haughton & Dutton's and the long looked for tools from Burditt & Williams. Sat up until 10 opening all of these treasures. Everything much admired. We have sprung suddenly from poverty into extreme opulence—almost luxury—but our fare being still confined to ham bacon & eggs we are not Sybarites[1].

Prayers, then bed 10:30, after arranging for the management of the boys—of which more hereafter.

WEDNESDAY JULY 5
Uncommonly cold last night so that we were all chilly even with 2 blankets each. Mosquitoes quiet in early part of night owing to our having established a smudge which nearly drove us out as well. Brisk & Julian up at 5:30 and proceeded to Sleeper's & Willoughby's for milk and eggs. Phil and E.P. took a much needed rest until 7: A.M. Breakfast eggs + bacon + with johnny cake[2] and coffee.
 Much activity this morning. Cleaning boats, clearing trees for a vista of the lake from the front

---

[1] *Sybarite is derived from the Greek Sybarites (see-va-REE-tees), from Sybaris, an ancient Greek city noted for the luxurious, pleasure-seeking habits of many of its inhabitants.*

[2] *A Johnycake is usually made of lightly sweetened cornmeal and hot water and fried in butter, somewhat*

Faculty Tents and main buiding

Out for a row—one of the main activities at G.S. Camp.

of the cabin, Setting cabins to rights, fixing flag staff & bathing. Fine day with good breeze. The Merry Andrew departed on a two hours' quest for potatoes—hence a late dinner—about 2 P.M.—and consequently fierce appetite. Dinner, ham, mashed potatoes & pie.

At 3:30 P.M. the 3 boats propelled by the different members of the faculty departed for the Landing place. After waiting an hour the boys turned up in charge of Mr. Thurston. Only seven came owing to a serious accident to one of the lads intending to come and this boy's chum stayed with him.

There arrived also Mr. Stanley—a young man who is working his way through college and into the Ministry. A very nice fellow who seems ready to help us in all ways. The boys, contrary to our expectation, exhibited no signs of shyness. They were almost uncomfortably cheerful, to the border of hilarity. As they hove in sight, the senior member of the Faculty was standing on the dock to receive them when he heard one of the youngsters ask J.M.G.—if "that was the cook"! They quickly established themselves in quarters, not having a superfluity of luggage.

First of all came the enrollment with addresses as follows:

Joseph Belyea *12 years*
4 Terrace Place *East Boston*

Edward Collings *13 years*
137 Princton St. *East Boston*

George A. Hatfield *14 years*
3 Boston Place *South Boston*

George King *11 years*
42 Cottage St. *East Boston*

Arthur Lee. *12 years*
528 Dorchester Ave. *South Boston*

George Orr *14 years*
112 West Ninth St. *South Boston*

Ernest Pope *13 years*
5 Union Court *East Boston*

Took them out for short row before tea but did not have them go into bathe, fearing fatigue

Washing clothes in lake

Rev. Endicott Peabody giving helping hand to a disabled camper.

after their long journey.

Tea 6 – Tomato soup, corn meal mush—boys not very hungry.

After Tea established following order of day, which unlike the laws of Medes & Persians[1] is liable to change.

5:45 A.M.	Mr. Stanley and 2 boys go ashore for milk at Willoughby's.
6:30 A.M.	Rising horn
6:45 .	Five minutes horn
7:00	Breakfast
7:30	Prayers in dining room or grove
7:45	Work cleaning up dormitory
	Work cleaning up dining room
	After that to 10.15 cleaning up grounds
10:30	Rowing or some other amusement & swimming
12:10	first horn for dinner
12:25	5 m. horn for dinner
12:30	Dinner
12:45-1:45	Reading
2:00	Rowing etc.
5:40	First horn for tea
5:55	5 m. horn for tea
6:00	Tea
6:30	
7:30	Amusement
7:45	Turn in
7:55	Prayers in Dormitory
8:00	Bed for boys—Mr. Stanley in charge & after 20 boys arrive 1 other of Faculty.

Rules:

    No boy bathe or go out in boat without some member of Faculty.
    No going into kitchen without Andrew's consent.
    Tools not to be touched.
    Boys to be marked each week and those who have best record
    (possibly others) will be invited again if the camp continues next
    year.

---

[1] *Your Majesty, you know a law of the Medes and Persians can never be changed. Daniel must be thrown into the lions' den!*

A short row before tea.

Laundry chores

Took all of them in 2 boats for a row around the islands.
Heavy thunder storm came up just after we landed. Boys rather lively in dormitory just before bed time. Quieted down at prayers. Faculty sat up till 10 playing dominoes and reading in dining room. Raining hard as we turned in –

THURSDAY, JULY 6
A fine day in spite of dark forebodings. Sunny with high wind. Faculty bathed. Boys found it a little chilly. They were rather cold in night. Perhaps better to break them in gradually & not have all windows open first night after their arrival. Much disturbance in morning owing to misunderstanding about time. Breakfast shortly after 7. Oatmeal, eggs and bacon – coffee for a few of boys – milk better for them. Clearing wood after chores. Boys did not set to work with a will, inclined to quarrel and shirk. Punished Belyea by not allowing him to go for row – thinking it well to start in at once - as the time for influencing them is short. P.L.S. and Stanley went off to Ashland in search of wood.

The rest of us in 2 boats moved to Balch's Camp[1] intending to bring over his scow – but the wind was too high. Bathed – all of us. Only 3 of these boys can swim, Dinner late, 12:30

In the afternoon a detachment went ashore to play ball.
East vs. South Boston. History does not record the score. Three boys, Lee, Pope and Orr, failing to obey Mr. Thurston, were not permitted to go out in boat that aft. or next morning before dinner. No news in papers as yet of the Harvard exams.

Large scow was brought over from Mr. Balch's camp – rather formidable for our present number, but it will prove useful by & by. At present our seven seem to be about 50. In the evening the boys tried fishing – Bed 8:15. The brethren listened long to the Merry Andrew's yarns. Reported to be thrilling & improbable. Bed for the rest at 9:45

FRIDAY, JULY 7
A different dormitory this morning from that of yesterday. Boys and Faculty silent and preoccupied until they were compelled to move by the senior member of Faculty. A lovely day—warmer than before, but not uncomfortable. Breakfast -oatmeal, ham and scrambled eggs. G.Z.G and T.P.T. rowed down to Holderness to see about stove. Returned in condition of much sunburn. The rest of us hauled boughs over to Island for a great bon-fire to welcome Mrs. Peabody on her arrival & chopped down more trees. Bathing just before dinner. Dinner good roast beef and plum pudding—of a simple nature. Boys do not eat much at present. Tendency on part of all to take rest after dinner. At 4, P.L.S., J.M.G. and E.P. took the Whitehall —henceforth to be known as "The Lady of the Nashua"—and rowed to the end of the Lake

---
[1] *Balch's Camp (Camp Chocorua), see next page.*

Ernest Balch And Camp Chocorua

CHOCORUA OCCUPIES AN IMPORTANT SPOT IN CAMPING HISTORY quite out of proportion to its short life of eight years (1880-1888). This was a small, specific purpose camp founded by Ernest Balch out of strong convictions and a missionary zeal, but with little money. Balch was concerned with "the miserable existence of wealthy adolescent boys in the summer when they must accompany their parents to fashionable resorts and fall prey to the evils of life in high society." This was in sharp contrast to his own life in New Hampshire, where he and his brothers were free to explore the countryside and master the lake. Something must be done, and he could and would do it!

By midwinter of his sophomore year at Dartmouth, Balch knew he had the answer. He would establish a camp for boys ages 12 to 16 years in the New Hampshire area he knew so well. The basic principles were clear in his mind, and he thought-out his plans very carefully. The indifference and ridicule of educators to whom he talked did not deter him. In late May Balch, his brother Stephen, and a friend set out to find a site in New Hampshire. Burnt Island in Squam Lake seemed ideal, so they immediately occupied it and started building a lodge. (Fortunately they were able to buy the island for 40 dollars when they were discovered by the startled owner.) Balch later reported that those June days were flat while they waited for the first rush of boys to appear. By mid-July a boy from Washington arrived, soon to be followed by his cousin. In late July three Boston boys joined the group. "We had a camp! My ideas were sound."

A young graduate student, C. E. Applegate, with whom Balch had camped, joined the faculty, and the plans began to be implemented. The aim was to develop hardy, responsible, independent, and resourceful youth. There would be no servants, no class distinctions, and no snobbery in this small, democratic, sharing community. An advertisement in the "Churchman" brought more boys the next year, and the camp grew steadily.

Students were divided into four rotating teams, supervised by faculty who, incidentally, were expected to do more than their share of the work. It was a busy life, with meals to be cooked in primitive fashion, dishes to be washed on the white sandy beach, waste to be fed daily to the fish, and grounds and quarters to be kept clean. Paths had to be cleared, and more huts built. A daily boat trip had to be made to town. Every boy was required to master the lake so as to move freely in safety and in any weather.

in order to inspect the cottage offered to Mr. Thayer by Shepherd Hill Hotel. Found it likely to prove a warm place & not altogether attractive. Quite an excitement to be among people again after our sojourn in the wilderness. Rowing back met Mr. DeMerritte who invited us to come to call upon him at Camp Algonquin a mile away. Found that the Brethren had been disporting themselves in boat races. Played dominoes and read until 9.45.

SATURDAY, JULY 8
Another glorious day. Rather cool last night. So that there was a tendency to avoid the morning plunge. But the weather outside was warmer than in the cabin and the bath was refreshing. Edward Collings had been refractory & was therefore in dormitory last night and was therefore forbidden to go in boats today. Lumber arrived last night and so P.L.S. and G.Z.G. set to work to complete the building they had started early in week. E.P. gave Stanley lesson in Greek. Rest chopping and clearing up. Tendency on the part of the boys to resist our wish for them to work—a tendency which we think well to counteract with considerable asperity. Next week we shall try marking the boys for work and conduct & giving most privileges to those who do best. In afternoon boys did a good deal of fishing, catching small fish, but none sufficient size to cook. Stanley, E.P., Hatfield and Pope rowed down to Meredith to get provisions. J.M.G. & Thurston drove to Ashland for stove pipe.

At early evening the Merry Andrew's long lost trunk turned up and he was happy once more. Cooking stove also arrived, but too late to be set up. An unusually sumptuous tea—Hash, prunes, johnny cake and doughnuts. In evening some checkers—mostly fishing.

After boys had retired Andrew regaled us with tales of his four shipwrecks which were especially interesting to one who like E.P., had just finished reading the "Wreck of the Grosvenor". Bed at 10. Heavy thunder storm which cleared away shortly after ten.

SUNDAY, JULY 9
Beautiful weather. Sunny with invigorating breeze. After chores accomplished had choir practice. Boys joined in fairly well. Sang "There Is A Green Hill," "The Church's One Foundation" & "Come My Soul." Sent over to Camp Algonquin to invite Mr. DeMerritt's boys to come to chapel. They rowed over—about 12 strong. Service in the beautiful little open air Church at Mr. Balch's Island. Service went well. E.P. preached short service on text "Speak, for thy Servant Heareth." Service about one hour. Rowed back at once. Allowed boys to bathe quietly. George Orr, Joseph Balyea to be on bounds tomorrow. After dinner T.P.T., Stanley and E.P. rowed over to Shepherd Hill House Landing and walked thence to call upon Mr. Allen at Bruce Piper's. Unfortunately he was out. Mrs. B.P. entertained them on the piazza & was original and entertaining. G.Z.G and P.L.S. rowed in White boat to Camp Asquam and went for

Winthrop T. Talbot & Camp Asquam

TAKING OVER CAMP HARVARD ON ASQUAM LAKE (across the lake and a few miles from Balch's Chocorua) in 1884, Winthrop Talbot established what Porter Sargent had called "the first commercially successful summer camp" (1935, p. 80). Talbot was the son of Dr. J. T. Talbot, dean of the Boston University Medical School. Winthrop became a doctor, too. Talbot's credentials as a professor of medicine at Boston University, a researcher, and community leader are excellent: he started the first course of pathology of blood ever given in the United States; helped establish the first commercial pasteurized milk route in Boston; developed the earliest successful application of alternating current to the shooting of X-rays.

All the work was done by the boys, and each day each camper had a different job. The assignment of tasks was done by what was termed by a past camper as a "rather unique bulletin board," suggesting this was the first "kaper" chart. (A "kaper" chart lists work responsibilities for campers.)

walk with Mr. Talbot[1] and his party. On being pressed to stay to tea they consented. Reported a much less formal condition of things at meals than with us. Boys went for walk on mountain with J.M.G and the M.A. In evening we all sat in dining room and sang hymns. Boys joined in with good deal of gusto.

MONDAY, JULY 10
Beautiful day. Very cold last night. Stanley went off at an early hour to look up tents, order blankets etc. in Boston. Usual routine at Camp. Chores chopping down trees and dragging boughs into scow. P.L.S and G.Z.G busy establishing a floor for the tents which we hope will some time come. Visited by a Mr. Cleveland & his party of three. After dinner Mr. Allen with his wife and 2 daughters came to see us. Photo'ed us all in the scow. E.P. took most of the boys for a berrying excursion on the mountain. Got raspberries and blueberries in some quantities but time was limited. Glorious view of lake from the hill. G.Z.G and P.L.S. made a sail which they used in "Lady of the Nashua." Boys tired in evening & glad to go to bed. So were we all—at 9:30.

TUESDAY, JULY 11
Another glorious day. Working busily most of morning—clearing and taking boughs in the scow over to the Island. J.M.G. and T.P.T. went for ice at Coolidge's Camp. Bathing at 11.30. After dinner, boys showed tendency to stay about house and rest. Telegram came from Mr. Thompson about Frank's exams. At 5, new boys arrived with Stanley. Had them come into dormitory and sit on benches until E.P. had registered them and instructed them in regard to their duties:

Harry E. Axan 12 years.
4 Beckler Ave.   *S. Boston*

Allen Breck 10 yrs
115 Webster St.   *E. Boston*

Joseph Dearden 13 yrs.
57 O Street.   *S. Boston*

Ralph H. Dixon 13 yrs.
2 Litchfield Court   *E. Boston*

Henry Gray 13 yrs.

---

[1] *Mr. Talbot directed nearby Camp Asquam. See next page.*

647 Saratoga St.   *E. Boston*

Charles Hansell 13 yrs.
309 Summer St.   *E. Boston*

James McLeod 12 yrs.
51 Jeffries St.   *E. Boston*

Hugh C. McMullen 12 yrs.
5 Swallow St.   *S. Boston*

Thomas W. Robinson 13 yrs.
754½ Sixth St.   *S. Boston*

John M. Sutcliffe   *S. Boston*

Re-distributed work giving old boys the pleasanter duties. Those who had behaved best having the easier assigned to them.

<u>Care of Boats</u> (Barret)—*Collings, King, Lee*

<u>Outside work</u>—(cleaning up including out house + tents) (Gray)
        Belyea, Hatfield, Orr,   *Pope*

<u>Dormitory</u>—   *Hansell, McLeod, McMullen,*   *Robinson, Sutcliffe*

<u>Dining Room</u>   *Axon, Breck, Dearden, Dixon, Gray*

New boys a likely looking lot and quieter than the first set. At tea they filled the room well. Had a subduing effect upon the old ones. After tea G.Z.G and E.P. took 3 new boys ashore in Lady of Nashua and waited for an hour for Cecil Barret, who had missed the 9 A.M. train from Boston. He was a welcome addition to our numbers. J.A. Sullivan who was due sometime this week not turned up.

WEDNESDAY, JULY 12
Fine day. The journal will be somewhat scanty for these next few days in as much as the journalist was called away after failing to record for a day or two. Consequence much mistiness in regard to details of the days. A boat went up to Whittens and in the afternoon there was a berrying party up the hill. Dearden decidedly homesick. He is apparently averse to work— a

Edwin Demerritte & Camp Algonquin

ANOTHER SCIENCE CAMP, CAMP ALGONQUIN, was in continuous existence from 1886 to 1929; it was directed by Edwin DeMerritte, who set high standards in nature appreciation. The camp was well-equipped with a nature library, microscope, herbarium, and a wild fern and flower garden. The boys made valuable lists of native flora and fauna. One wonders what Joseph Rothrock's reaction would have been to this camp director who so nearly followed his own botanical interests, yet each was unknown to the other.

DeMerritte felt that "a camp should be educational, not only in the development of character, but also in a close study of all that God created for our enjoyment." He was consistent in his beliefs and at a testimonial dinner upon the occasion of his eighty-third birthday reiterated his ambition as "to reach boys through teaching; to mold them into men of stamina; men of character; to create in them a definite aim in life; to give them a conception of their Maker through an understanding of nature."

DeMerritte taught for many years at Chauncey Hall School in Boston, was later principal of the Berkeley Preparatory School, and when he retired he was head of his own school. As an educator he placed emphasis on reading and exposing boys to the sound principles of work as the law of life and love of work as the joy of life. He was one of that group of men to convene in 1903 at the camp conference in Boston. Gibson's history (1936) pointed out the longevity of early camping pioneers and the fact that Balch, Hinkley, and DeMerritte (then age 90) were all living in 1936, "their interest in the education and the advancement of youth undimmed."

spoilt child and might be omitted from next years company.

THURSDAY, JULY 13
Work going on busily upon the floor for the tents. In the afternoon Julian drove E.P. with 2 boys to Ashland. There the 4:20 P.M. train was missed. And so the unfortunate gentleman had to take 4:07 next morning. This evening Mr. DeMerritte[1] was out fishing with young Dunton & by accident dory was overturned & Dunton drowned after De Merritte had struggled long to save him. De Merritte landed at our Island and was rowed back by Briskie. The brethren rowed about the Island where the accident occurred for a long time, but as no one came out they rowed home. A feeling of sadness pervaded the camp that night. Fortunately the boys did not learn of it.

FRIDAY JULY 14
Fine day. Warm. Phil Smith after a short and hurried piece of working in morning rushed off to his train. Platform for tents completed and 2nd tent put up in evening. Mrs. Peabody and and Frank Thompson returned with E.P. on 1 P.M. train from Boston reaching camp at 7o'clock. Brethren had been dragging lake—but all to no purpose. Great bonfire on Burnt Island in honor of Mrs. P.

SATURDAY JULY 15
Fine. E.P. called on Mr. De Merritt— found him in a sad condition. Brethren dragged Lake. Body was found at 11 o'clock – a good deal disfigured. It was taken up to Ashland at once. E.P. took crew of 8 boys up to Squam Bridge and got a dory which took back in tow. In P.M. great game of baseball ashore   - East vs. South Boston - much excitement. Boat race coming home.

SUNDAY JULY 16
Fine - high wind. At 9:15 set out for church at Shepherd Hill - whole company in 4 boats. After rounding Mooney's Point came into teeth of sharp wind with high seas. J.M.G. and F.G..T. in Lady Of Nashua had to take dory in tow. Rest had rather hard time of it. Reached Church just little late. Excellent discourse from Mr. Sprague on "He toucheth the mountains and they smoke".
Coming home an easier matter. Swim and then dinner at 2:30. Boys rather quiet in P.M. Went for short walk ashore. G.Z.G and J.M.G. sailed up to Asquam for tea. Mr. de Merritt and 10 of his company came to sing hymns in evening. <u>Recommended</u> that they & all camps be invited to join us on Sunday evenings. Prayers followed.

---

[1] *Mr. Edwin DeMerritte and Camp Algonquin, see page opposite.*

The Reverend Endicott Peabody Presiding over the Camp (1890s - artist unknown)

MONDAY JULY 17

Dull in morning. Warm with slight rain - At 10:10 E.P. and Frau departed and here endeth E.P.'s jurisdiction - G.Z. Gray left in charge - & he is herein to keep a true & careful record.

Avove, a turn-of-the-century postcard showing St. Peters In The Mount Episcopal Church on Shepherd Hill Rd. Holderness.

The church is now a well kept private residence. Courtesy of Larry Mowbray..

GROTON SCHOOL CAMP — 1893 JOURNAL

Chop wood-carry water.

G. S. Camp boys showing off 3 pots of berries picked on the mountain.

GROTON SCHOOL CAMP — 1893 JOURNAL

The Halcyon Steam Boat at the Bridge

All in for a swim!

GROTON SCHOOL CAMP — 1893 JOURNAL

Ice Harvesting

By Debra Cottrell

Harvesting natural ice became big business in New England during the 19th century. The birth of America's large scale commercial ice industry began in New England in 1805. Frederick Tudor, a Boston merchant, created the first natural ice business in the United States. He shipped ice harvested on a pond in Lynn Massachusetts to the West Indies. Over the next thirty years Tudor made a fortune shipping ice around the world to places like Charleston, New Orleans, Cuba, Calcutta, South America, China and England. British records show that Queen Victoria purchased some ice from Massachusetts in the 1840's.

Nathaniel Jarvis Wyeth, one of Tudor's ice harvesting foreman developed many specialized tools such as plows and saws to improve the harvesting of ice. In 1858, the Tudor company expanded their harvesting operations to Milton, New Hampshire. Ice was harvested in the winter and stored in huge ice houses to allow for year round distribution. During the summer months, special ice trains carried, on the average, fifty cars a day from Milton. In 1880, the Wakefield, New Hampshire area followed suit and opened the Independent and Driver's Union Ice companies.

G.S. Camp Staff lifting ice using ice tines and block & tackle.

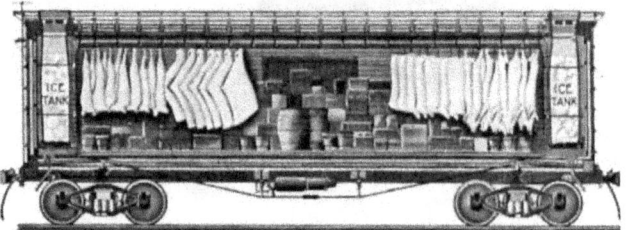

The Camp bought ice from the local ice house on Squam. Mechanical refrigeration was not available then.

Chapter 8

July 17 - July 25

1893

By

G. Z. Gray

GROTON SCHOOL CAMP — 1893 JOURNAL

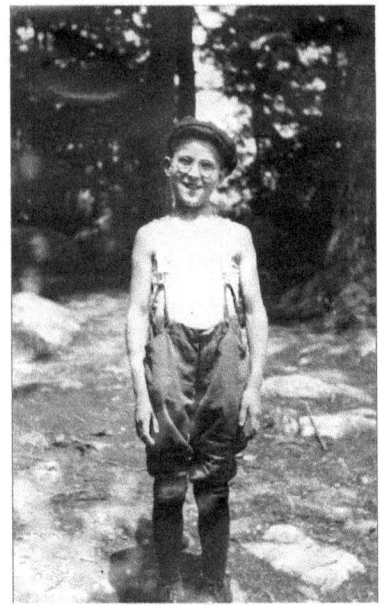

MONDAY, JULY 17

REV. PEABODY AND OUR FAIR VISITOR[1] having departed, and the appropriate parting salutes having been given, work was again resumed. The "lawn" was raked, the ice was stored, the boats cleaned, etc. Before dinner Dearden had another fit of homesickness which he called a stomach ache so he was put to bed, and gave him plenty of ginger to prevent him the opportunity of calling his trouble by the same name a second time. C.B., T.P.T. and Robinson returned late for dinner from Whittiers and smarting muchly from sun burn. After dinner a rain sprang up, and all were driven in-doors where Sutcliffe gave a really wonderful exhibition of tumbling; this time his body in all sorts of shapes, and dancing the Highland Fling, Sword Dance etc. Next the boys went fishing but the rain did not help their luck. The scow was filled and taken to the little island to be dumped but as there was not time to finish the work it was dropped. There were present at supper two guests from Camp Asquam who hereto affix their names -

Karl Ohnesorg - Camp Asquam
John Mason Parker - Camp Asquam

Two visitors from Willoughby's came in the evening, and all separated at about half past nine under the mutterings of a coming thunderstorm—cards and then bed by 10.

TUESDAY, JULY 18

This morning we have (as usual) a lovely day for the boys to return to their homes. The whole of the first batch left with the exception of Arthur Lee who is to stay another week. His two weeks have made him much stronger and, as he has been a good boy it was decided to keep him in the place of Joe Dearden, whose homesickness and discontent culminated in his departure with the others this morning. The boys went away under the care of Briskie and Jule so that for the minute we felt quite lonely. During the morning our visitors from Willoughby's again came and stayed for a perfect age. Andrew accidentally poured some boiling water on Tom Robinson's hand but a speedy application of soda relieved the pain. It will probably be perfectly well in a few days. After dinner a bonfire was used to burn up the leaves etc. collected in the morning. T. Thurston, Uligs and Kil then made an expedition to the little island to bale out the scow. In the midst of this exceedingly dirty and wet occupation Mr. Sturgis and the new batch of boys arrived.

Nine new boys under escort of S.W.S. arrived in fairly good spirits after a very dirty journey, during the course of which considerable insight into the character of the nine was obtained. There was a divided desire to swear at "hay-seeds" by the wayside. The following are the newcomers.

---

[1] *Mrs. Peabody*

Indian Mush *(Corn meal hasty pudding)*
Recipe

Have ready on a clear fire, a pot of boiling water. Stir into it, by degrees, (a handful at a time,) sufficient Indian meal to make a very thick porridge, and then add a very small portion of salt, allowing not more than a level tea-spoonful to a quart of meal. You must keep the pot boiling all the time you are stirring in the meal; and between every handful stir hard with the mush-stick, (a round stick about half a yard long, flattened at the lower end,) as, if not well stirred, the mush will be lumpy. After it is sufficiently thick and smooth, keep it boiling an hour longer, stirring it occasionally. Then cover the pot closely, and hang it higher up the chimney, or set it on hot coals on the hearth, so as to simmer it slowly for another hour. The goodness and wholesomeness of mush depends greatly on its being long and thoroughly boiled. It should also be made very thick. If well made, and well cooked, it is wholesome and nutritious; but the contrary, if thin, and not sufficiently boiled. It is not too long to have it three or four hours over the fire, first boiling, and then simmering. On the contrary it will be better for it. The coarser the corn meal the less cooking it requires. Send it to the table hot, and in a deep dish. Eat it with sweet milk, buttermilk, or cream; or with butter and sugar, or with butter and molasses; making a hole in the middle of your plate of mush; putting some butter into the hole and then adding the sugar or molasses.

Cold mush that has been left, may be cut into slices, or mouthfuls, and fried the next day, in butter, or in nice drippings of veal, beef, or pork; but not mutton or lamb.

(From Eliza Leslie's Lady's New Recipe Book, 1848)
http://www.journalofantiques.com

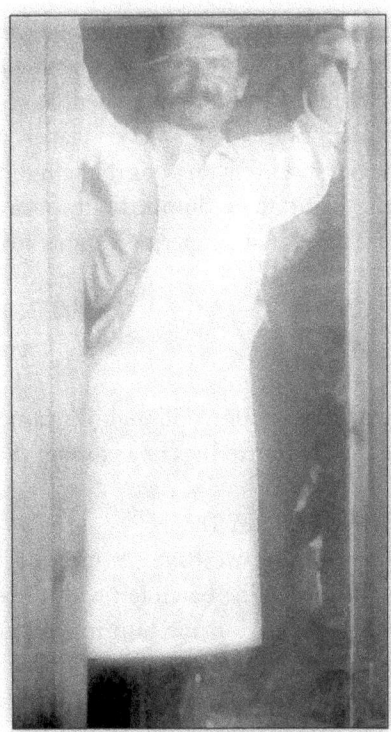

First G.S. Camp Chef, "The Merry Andrew"

John Rice - 11 yrs   *3 Cusson Pl.*
George Rice - 9 yrs   *Boston*
Angelo Piotti - 12 yrs   *11 So. Margin St.*
Luigi Piotti - 10 yrs   *11 So. Margin St.*
Julius Gerwain - 12 yrs   *731 Parker St.*
Harold Johanson - 14 yrs   *1 Maldin Ct.*
Segurd Bromwell - 11 yrs   *97 E. Lenox St. Boston*
Ralph Patrick - 9 yrs   *c/o Sister Dorothy*
Allen Mower - 12 yrs   *20 Allen St. W. Cambridge*

Showed the boys their quarters and then put them in the lake to wash. The orderly and obedient behavior of the older set quieted them considerably, and there was no grumbling, tho' Signor Angelo was troubled by the lack of a pillow. Our first experience of the "Merry Andrew's" skill was vastly satisfactory. Indian-mush, johnny-cake, apple-sauce and doughnuts made a first-class supper. Then some took a short row, while others were getting the new boys broken into their duties. Prayers at 8:15 and bed for the boys. Andrew's interest in cards kept the "officers" as he calls us, up till 10:30. Mr. Robinson and H. Clews and Williams joined our force in the afternoon.

WEDNESDAY, JULY 19
The faculty occupied their tents last night for the first time and slept beautifully, notwithstanding warnings about hard cots and few blankets. Breakfast over, work was in order, and before 10:30 we had made a creditable attack upon the piles of cut brushwood. About 9 Robinson and Clews left for a sail, and we saw no more of them till 6 hrs. later. Took half of the boys to the beach, while the rest bathed here. Luigi, the youthful Italian bathed in his own fashion, which was not ours; result, bounds for Luigi.
P.M. Adjourned to mainland for ball, leaving the two Rices and Luigi on the island because of disobedience. Judging by excitement of the players the game was one of fierce interest. G.R. and H.C. returned by land, about 9 P.M. and then started for their boat, which they had left after a brisk sail before the wind. She refused to beat back, and they refused to row back till the winds moderated. This it did towards evening and they got back to supper, boat and all. Mr. DeMerritte called in the afternoon, and in the evening three gentlemen from Willoughby's dropped in for a chat. George Rice was talked to and punished for swearing—promised amendment. Bed at 10 o'clock. New boys have done pretty well for the first day. Angelo a treasure in the kitchen.

THURSDAY, JULY 20
The finest kind of weather, bright and fresh. Waked by songs of thrushes and warblers, to another day of active pleasure. Organized a fishing squad under Clews, which started for Balch's

The Steamer Kusumpe, shown above, is named after the Lake. Originally, they referred to Squam as keeseenunknipee, which meant "the goose lake in the highlands". The white settlers that followed shortened the name to Casumpa, Kusumpy and/or Kusumpe around 1779. In the early 1800s, the lake was given another Abenaki name, Asquam, which means water. Finally, in the early 1900s, Asquam was shortened to its present version, Squam.

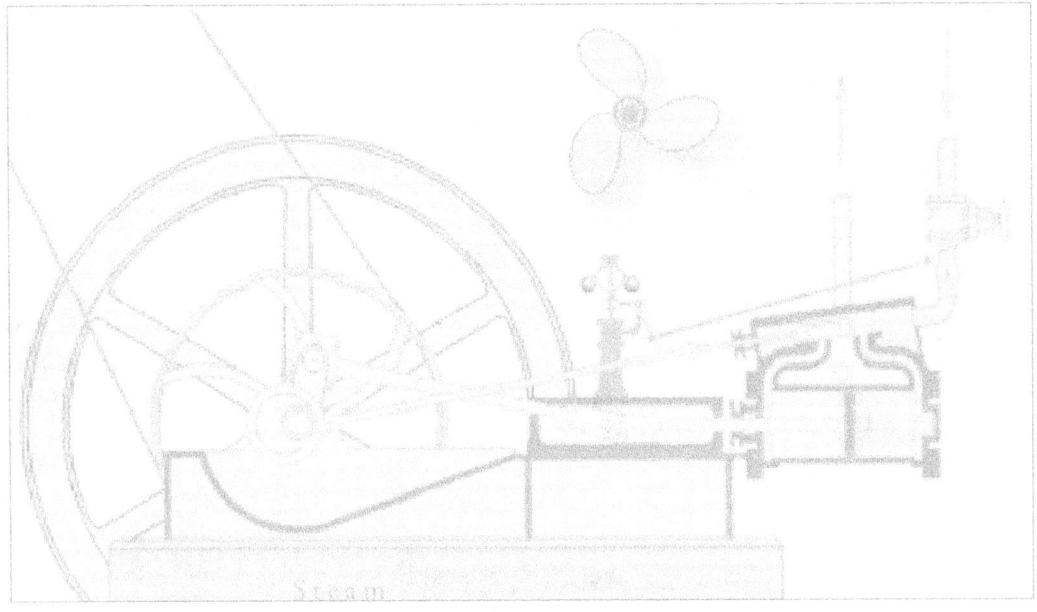

Island soon after breakfast. The Merry Andrew turned himself into a barber's shop and clipped Jim Rice. Fishing squad returned with 9 small perch. After dinner, L. Thomson and S.W.S. with a kid-crew got a load of ice, and then everyone went berrying on hills near Harpers. Came back with 6 quarts of blue and rasp-berries. Found our fire was traveling underground, and was liable to get away from us, so we set to work and dumped water on it by the barrelful. It still smoldered in places but seemed beyond doing any harm. In the evening Clew's crew won a close and well-rowed race from Barrets.' T.P.T. and Stanley went to supper with Mr. Allen and we sat up for them till 11 o.c. Andrew then served us with cheese sandwiches and doughnuts, which closed a satisfactory day. Had a call about noon from Maj. Gibbs, Barrets' Uncle, in a steam launch.

FRIDAY, JULY 21
The faculty and boys bade a sad farewell this morning to the genial 'Clews', Mr. R. driving him to Ashland. Another fishing expedition resulted in absolutely nothing, the trouble being too hot sun I think. We must try it in early morning or evening. Work for the boys was a little irregular, because the faculty was busy moving and improving their tents. The Kusumpe steamer arrived with lumber for new piazza, and barrels for float. Allen Mower is homesick, probably because he usually goes to the country in summer and it is therefore an old story to him. Expected the steamer in afternoon to take us around the lake, a trip offered us by Maj. Gibbs. She did not appear and we went ashore for baseball. Williams and Sturgis found their task as captains, umpires and peacemakers rather difficult; and the latter finally resigned his position and brought the grumblers back to camp. Under head-carpenter Barret we made a fair start on the new dining room piazza. After tea Barret and S.W.S. called on Mr. DeMerritte's camp. Our usual visitors from Willoughby's spent most of the evening with us. Boys all well. Andrew rejoices that tomorrow gives him a new kitchen squad. Luigi and the Rices are not much use to him. In the excitement of a close race between the boats, Mr. Barret twisted his ankle. He bore the pain with equanimity, but not so the gibes of our merry cook. The ankle recovered quickly, and will give no trouble.

SATURDAY, JULY 22
This morning there were lowering clouds which seemed to promise a wet day at last. The new piazza occupied C.B. and T.P.T. practically all day and by night they could view the finished work with proud satisfaction. The boys worked pretty steadily till 11 o.c. While I was at the beach with the bathers, a Mr. Cleveland and friends from Boston called. I was returning in usual working costume, on a raft which we found at the beach; which some of the boys fortunately warned me of our visitors. So I landed at back of our tents, and secured more ample clothing. During dinner the clouds gave way and the camp had a drenching. The steamboat trip had of course to be postponed again. Tried fishing when the rain stopped, but caught nothing large. The boys were happy, and enjoyed a short drill which Thurston gave them. This might prove

Asquam Lake House

Campers on Island dock

a good thing every day, as inculcating ideas of discipline. After tea they played a complicated species of leap-frog which was well worth watching. I tried them at blind man's buff, but it proved a failure. The one who was "it" wrestled sturdily with all who came near him, being careful not to hold anyone; while all the others hustled and punched him in vain efforts to be caught. Now at 8:30 P.M. Moncuri is taking cooking lesson from Andrew with enthusiastically polite interest. Barret and S.P.S. have gone on a potato hunt to Whiteman's.

SUNDAY, JULY 23
The weather cleared last night and today began clear with high wind. So high was the wind that we hesitated at first about rowing to church. The wind moderated however, and we went in 4 boats, borrowing Harper's dory. The boys behaved well, and we returned to dinner at 1:30. Clouds had risen quickly and we were caught 5 minutes from shore in a heavy rain. Andrew's warm soup, soon took the chill out of us, and the rest of the dinner was equally agreeable, consisting of lamb, potatoes, beets, custard and doughnuts. Messrs. Barret, Thurston and Williams stayed to dinner at the Asquam House. The afternoon passed quickly in reading, writing and a short walk with about half the boys. Clews started away under Moncuri's escort at 4 o'clock. It is a pity he had to leave just as he was getting into the swing. The second week is bound to be the better and more effective of the two. Maj. Gibbs asked whether we clothed our boys, a compliment to their Sunday costumes. After tea I read "The Little Duke" aloud with partial success, after which Piotti Sr. told a fairy tale to a circle of entranced listeners. Then we sang hymns for half an hour and dispersed at 8:30.

MONDAY, JULY 24
Cool and as the boys w'ld say, "more than windy." A good morning's work in general cleaning up. Williams and S.W.S. made a laborious trip for ice, and decided that in future something must be contrived to carry the ice in, and save the boats. After dinner there was anxious watching for the promised steamboat, enlivened by excitement over some photographs of groups by S.W.S. At the first whistle of the boat, wild cheering was started for Major Gibbs, the steamer, engineer, pilot and the Camp. We embarked, cheering Stanley who stayed at home and cut down the much feared bee-tree. When Luigi "the young shreny" was dressed for the occasion, his trousers set rather strangely upon him, and they were found to be on wrong side before. Our steamer went the length of the lake, and then wound thru' a narrow channel into Squaw Cove. Here we landed and rejoiced in excellent ice-cream and cake. Returned at 5:30 highly delighted with the excursion, and with Maj. Gibbs kindness. After supper the faculty reclined upon the new piazza and enjoyed a variety show by the kids, in which John Sutcliff's grace, Harry Gary's sand, and Luigi's monkey shine were about equally prominent. Mr. R. gone to bed early with a cold. Glorious moonlight over the water. Started custom of an evening hymn at prayers.

NEARER, MY GOD, TO THEE

Words: Sarah Adams, 1841.
Music: Lowell Mason, 1856.

Nearer, my God, to Thee, nearer to Thee!
E'en though it be a cross that raiseth me,
Still all my song shall be, nearer, my God, to Thee.

>   Nearer, my God, to Thee,
>   Nearer to Thee!

Though like the wanderer, the sun gone down,
Darkness be over me, my rest a stone.
Yet in my dreams I'd be nearer, my God to Thee.

There let the way appear, steps unto Heav'n;
All that Thou sendest me, in mercy given;
Angels to beckon me nearer, my God, to Thee.

Then, with my waking thoughts bright with Thy praise,
Out of my stony griefs Bethel I'll raise;
So by my woes to be nearer, my God, to Thee.

Or, if on joyful wing cleaving the sky,
Sun, moon, and stars forgot, upward I'll fly,
Still all my song shall be, nearer, my God, to Thee.

There in my Father's home, safe and at rest,
There in my Savior's love, perfectly blest;
Age after age to be, nearer my God to Thee.

"Nearer, My God, to Thee" was sung at the end of the 1936 movie San Francisco, which was nominated for several Academy Awards. It is also played by the ship's band in Titanic, winner of the Academy Award for best picture of 1997.

There are also many inspiring true life stories associated with this hymn. Some Titanic survivors said it was played by the ship's

TUESDAY, JULY 25

General excitement in camp over departure of boys. Allen Mower went with them, being homesick and anxious to leave. Decided to keep John Sutcliff another week, influenced by his paleness and his good behavior. Dispatched a sworn letter to T. Hale who wrote to say he must give up the camp. The boys went off under Barret's escort amid sincere regrets. Chorus was distinguished by usual success with Luigi, who worked perhaps a quarter of the time. About dinner-time rain set in and continued till night. The head of the Commissariat went off on an excursion and returned minus half his beautiful locks. The boys played ball over the steps, and some even lay on their cots and slept awhile. The rain interfered with assignments ashore. At 4 o.c. in a heavy rain J.S.D. Codiman turned up with ten boys as follows:

Waldo Herbert Jones - 12 yrs.   *4 Buckingham Pl.*
Israel Bean - 13 yrs.   *8 Billerica St.*
Nicholas Roghaar - 13 yrs.   *32 Grunswick St.*
Thomas Grisswood - 11 yrs.   *1 Dickinson St.*
Jeremiah Sullivan - 14 yrs.   *137 Beach Street*
Arthur Gray - 13 yrs.   *70 E. Windsor St.*
Wm. Barker -14 yrs.   *45 Utica St.*
Charles Barker - 12 yrs.   *45 Utica St.*
Wm. Carroll - 13 yrs.   *33 Crimson Pl.*
Ernest Cameron - 13 yrs.   *69 Warwick St.*

These new guests after registering at headquarters went to the dormitory and put on dry things. They seem a promising lot, older and more responsible than our last. Just after tea the welcome arrival of Benedict was announced. He relieves Williams in dormitory. The latter takes outdoor squad, Moncuri kitchen, and Codiman boats. While the faculty was playing casino, Stanley came in with news of a new boy walking in his sleep. Young Jones had walked till forcibly stopped by the wall. After consultation we strapped him in, to wait till morning, in bed. At prayers the boys sang "Nearer my God to Thee" with good effect.

Chapter 9

July 26 - August 5

1893

By

E. S. Benedict

Camper John Sutcliffe, above far right, will stay an extra week

Cots made from wood frame & canvas provided big heap'm—sleep'm.

Wednesday, July 26

THE MORNING WAS OVERCAST with same from 10 o' clock. Got in 2 hrs. work on the ground and Pioti Jr. was put on bounds for jumping on cots, declined to take his breakfast. He was boycotted by the faculty in hopes of touching his pride by lack of notice. Results not apparent. J.P.S had an excellent half hr. of drill in which new boys were good. Altogether they are a good lot. After dinner the weather cleared, and a hot ball-game was contested, the best on record. No kicking, great interest, and score a tie at 19-19. It is advised that the faculty take an active part in those games. After prayers, Messrs. and R. Gray called from Camp Chocorua and spent a half hr. in boats watching the moon and brilliant lightning as rival attractions. Tremendous thunder clouds passed over but without rain.

Thursday, July 27

Weather threatening all day, but no rain. Work till 10:30, then a half hr. of drill, which seems a good institution. It is extremely hard to keep the brethren steadily at work for three hours, and the drill, tho the phasing is distinctly educational. It is worth a good deal to see Capt G.P.G paralyzing glance fixed full upon Luigi for 30 seconds together. Luigi is paralyzed while the glance remains. Major Gibbs put the finishing touch to his kindness by sending today a large American flag with a check for $25.00 to erect a suitable pole, the bal. to go towards general camp fund. He also sent a number of printed cards containing patriotic songs. <u>P.M. Messers.</u> Armistad, Robinson and Thurston went calling at Asquam house, while another lively ball-game took place on shore. In the evening, had a visit from Messr's Talbot & Stanton—council members of Camp Asquam. Invited us to their aquatic sports tomorrow at 10 A.M. and asked J.S.C. and G.P.G and L.W.L. to act as judges. John Rice again talked to seriously and put him on bounds for Ralph Patrick's foot, which he cut 2 days ago with a hatchet, which is healing well. Prompt measures must be taken to build new Wharf. The present one is liable to collapse at any moment. By some stupid carelessness the present chronicler forgot to record an interesting event last Thursday, which must not be lost to history. The boats were away and Brother Robinson, having finished his daily bulletin of Henry C's moral and physical condition was fearful that we would miss our next "hourly" mail. He therefore disrobed and swam ashore and sped swiftly down the highroad towards the mailbox. A rumble tells of approaching vehicle, and into the woods darts Loring. Alas! He hides back of watering trough and the wagoner hauls up to refresh his beasts [horses]. Imagine the situation of our sensitive friend, crouching among the bushes and in terrible fear of discovery and capture as an escaped lunatic. The horses sniffed uneasily causing fresh palpitation but finally the agony ended and Robinson returned, weak but thankful for their escape.

Friday, July 28

Went in two boats with the 9 older boys to Camp Asquam at 10 A.M. Enjoyed the exhibition of swimming greatly, and Messrs, Codman and Sturgis judged the events with great satisfaction to themselves. Stan & boys caught 30 good perch before breakfast, which supplied our dinner.

The "ARK" with Crew (Whitehall Boat)—1896

Aroused by a tearful complaint from Israel Brown, who stated that some one had "punched the blood out of his lip." When asked if it hurt, he said no and went off contented with a word of sympathy.

P.M Took 16 boys with Ken and Billy for an ascent of Rattlesnake Mtn. The climb is not hard, but Gray (known as "flat" or "Slim") required a good deal of urging to keep them at it. A good view from the top, of Squam & Winnipesauke Lakes. Jerry Sullivan inquired with some alarm on our way down what it was that was growling. I assured him that the animals there were generally harmless. After tea the faculty minus Williams, and L.W. L., went off to a social event at Camp Asquam. At prayers, Luigi was missing, after anxious search he was found in a wooden box, which he had crawled into. Andrew rowed out on a lake entertained us with a variety of songs, yodels and trumpet calls till bed time. Others returned at 12.

SATURDAY, JULY 29
Rained steadily all the morning. Boys rather noisy, but cheerful. Fred reading aloud one of Hunty's books, but Luigi then Tom distracted attention of the others. I request to record that after repeated disobedience on the formers part, I lost my temper and gave the little rascal, one solid spank. Tears, anger, a talk, followed. Perhaps my wrath may prove well-timed, anger, a talk assured pertinence and reconciliation trimmed. Thurston drove [boat, then horse & buggy] to Ashland [Train Station] for shopping, and to meet David Bigwood who was left behind last Sunday. Arrived about 4:o'clock with the youth, who registers as follows:

David Bigwood 11yrs   *13 Greenville Place, Boston*

Afternoon uneventful. Evening the faculty, with exception of L.W.L. departed for the Asquam House. A perfectly still night, full moon, and clear sky, as I write an unwell screech owl was giving his unearthly yell not 50 ft from the tent. Waldo Jones went to bed unwell, the result probably of a bath this afternoon. Could not make him take a dose of Jamaica Ginger. The rest came back at 1 A.M.

SUNDAY, JULY 30
 A lovely day. Practiced hymns at 10, and service at 11 in Chocorua Chapel. About 60 people there and we had a delightful service. Mr. Allen talked most appropriately on the text, "The Lord Is Loving Unto Every Soul And His Mercy Is Over All His Works." It was a simple representation of God in his beautiful works of nature and the boys listened well. Mr. & Mrs. Allen returned with us to dinner, a triumph of Andrew's skill. Boys bathed at beach. Four did not go to church including Bean (Jewish) and R.Sullivan (Catholic). Sure their parents objected. Greenwoods and C. Barker stayed unnecessarily, they had better go next Sunday.

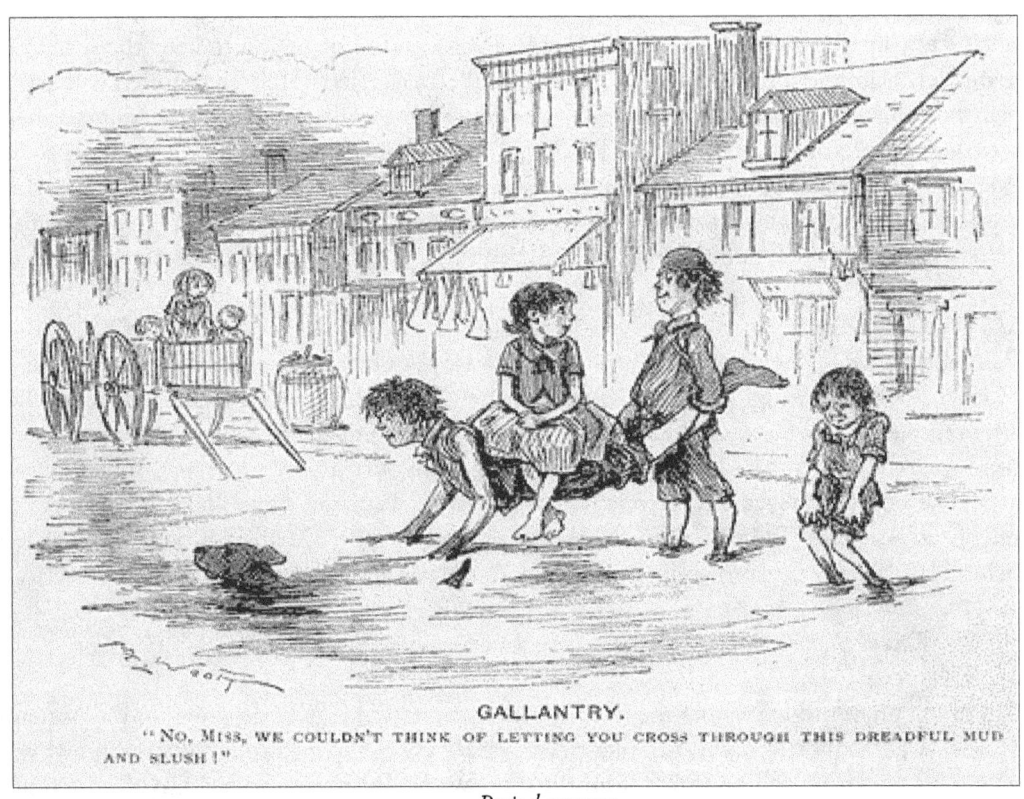

Period cartoon

Lunch and then two boys rowed to the Allens home after dinner, which most of the others went ashore for a walk. At prayer time sang hymns. H. Coolidge called, and about 10 o'clock under his guidance, J.L.C and L.C. L. started for a visit to the haunted house on Long Island under the ghostly light of the moon They softly entered Dead Man's Cove, crept thru an obscure path and suddenly came upon the house. Rickety and rotten, hidden among thick growth on all sides, and the scene of an atrocious murder in bygone yrs. It seemingly has a right to be haunted .

MONDAY, JULY 31
A beautiful day. After a good morning's work had an "other than fine" bath and swim at the beach. In the afternoon, went in a body to Long Isle. for blueberries... when boys returned with M.R. & L.W.L they brought home a load of ice and Thurston & Stanley went to Whitten's for provisions. After tea there was several short but extremely close and exciting races between chosen crews under Grossman, Williams Benedict and Luigi are having their last day. John Rice on bounds for lying.

TUESDAY, AUG 1
Parted from Piotti, Rice and Co. this morning in a decidedly wet rain. Grossman. Codman, Robinson & Williams went with the boys. Very sorry to lose Angelo and Siguered and Sutcliffe, but the others leave no great regret behind them. We who were left went to work with a will on the new wharf, and made a fair start before dinner. A pouring rain stopped work in the afternoon, and at 4 o'clock G.P.G & L.P. L. went to landing to wait for the new arrivals. They came about 5 o'clock having waited in a barn during the rain. P. Whitney, H.R. Richards and W.L. Cutting brought these boys;

Theodore Gossofard 13 yrs	*21 Prescott St.,*	*Charlestown*
Wm. Gardener 11 yrs	*13 Pearl St.,*	*Charlestown*
John Copitorn 10 yrs	*5 George St.,*	*Boston*

Finished and with the new flag-pole prone upon the ground. Took tea at Camp Chocorua and discussed situations with H. Coolidge with regard to next year's camp. Rather came to conclusion that we could not better our current position. On reaching camp at prayer time I found Waldo Jones wailing over a sore eye punched by Sonny Greenwood, and White again wailing to go home. Promised to take the latter tomorrow if he did not think better of it in the morning. Faculty agreed that we cannot waste our energies in keeping boys against their will, who talk of starting for Boston on foot, with 50 cents in their pocket. Whitney and Cutting went fishing at 10 P.M for hornpout. The result must be reported by another hand, for the permanent director for the faculty must now close his journal, after narration of a letter from

Chocorua Island is the site of America's first resident boys' summer camp. established in 1881 by Mr. Ernest Balch, the Camp operated until 1889.

R ELIGIOUS SERVICES WERE A VITAL PART OF THE CAMP'S ACTIVITY. In 1903 a group of Mr. Balch's relatives and former campers organized the Chocorua Chapel Association "for the purpose of religious services according to the form of the Protestant Episcopal Church." Mr. Clinton Crane, the owner of the island, made it available for worship services and in 1928 he generously donated it to the Association for that sole purpose.

For 38 years, Dr. Clifford Twombly, one of the founders of the Association, conducted services. Since 1941, they have been led by clergy of various denominations, many being summer residents of the Squam area. A list of preachers and pictures of the original boys' summer camp are in the Memorial Book near the entrance to the chapel.

Harry Gray to Stanley. In it he regretted delay in writing, and explained it by saying that "whenever he thought of it, it went out of his mind." I now hand over my pen to E.L. Benedict, until the arrival of Wm. Woods.

WEDNESDAY, AUG 2 *(No entry)*

THURSDAY, AUG 3
Mr. Sturgis departs to the slow music of a alarm clock, snores and other lamentations at half past four this morning. The writer heard the beginning of the alarm but its gentle tone lulled him to slumber again and he was unable to speed the parting host. Whitney comes in at half past six after a night of sleeplessness and torture. Some kids had the nightmares and others begged for his blankets. To cap the climax one took his bed without asking permission. All this much pleased the former monitor. After breakfast and awful two hours of work followed. We emptied the scow! The faculty—as well as the kids—were conspicuous by their absence when it came time for this operation. Basker and Jerry Sullivan surprised every one by the amount of work done. No one has been able to account for it yet. Most of the new boys acted like spoiled children and were afraid to dirty their hands. When the work is finished treasurer and secretary Thurston crawls out of his hole looking much the worse for the fight. He acknowledges that his mental faculty was unequal to the task of squaring accounts and he was 1.98 ½ short. By lunch time however it was discovered that the account loss was an unpaid bill of Robinson's. After this Secretary Thurston relaxes the cases of his position by joining the kids in a game of ball. Then some ladies arrive and Secretary Thurston tried to hide behind his beard as he is on the raft in his negligee. A flight to the shore and subsequent appearance of the Secretary. Whitney and Benedict have also improved their time elsewhere and arrive in camp late for tea (as usual) added by Sec. Thurston, Mr. Woods does arrive and a night of anxiety is booked for the faculty.

FRIDAY, AUG 4
Early morning fishing tempted four members of the faculty out on the like at four A.M this morning. The sunrise was beautiful and one of the boats had good luck, but there were a good many yawns indulged in before bed time by the enthusiastically spontaneous? After breakfast the new boys grew sulky when called upon to work and expressed their opinions rather freely about the unpleasantness of camp life. These boys seem a pampered set who expect everything done for them without doing anything in return. A more dreary morning for the gentleman in charge of the outside squad has not often been passed. About noon fellows from the Chocorua Camp came for the scow and we had to undue most of our mornings work. It was surprising the difference in time between the two operations. Just after this excitement had passed we were still more agitated by the appearance of Mrs. Bishop and daughter and Miss Forbes from the Asquam House. This event seemed to interest several of the younger members of the

GROTON SCHOOL CAMP — 1893 JOURNAL

faculty greatly, especially where one of them discovered that the visitors had brought six boxes of marshmallows as a present. They were escorted over to the camp and then back to shore in a short time as we did not see our way clear to inviting them to lunch. In the afternoon came the usual ball game and at four o'clock the long expected and much wished for Mr. Woods arrived to take charge of the camp and this diary. And here ended the second and last attempt of E.S. Benedict to write a camp journal.

SATURDAY, AUGUST 5
Cloudy weather all the morning threatening rain, but a fine afternoon. Tommy Greenwood and Nicholas Roghaart owned up to stealing cigarettes from the Andrew, and were put on bounds indefinitely, with the understanding that good behavior would lesser the punishment. Greenwood seems a rather bad lot. Mill Carroll stole raisins, grounded for the day. Jones and Gray were kept in for swimming without permission yesterday. Altogether there were too many punished boys in the camp for a healthy tone. The faculty put in a good morning work on the new wharf, getting the framework set up. At eleven the free boys went over to Sandy Beach swimming, and after dinner they went to play ball leaving the A.N.W. in change of the prisoners at the camp.

As it happened, the prisoners had a very good time, as the campers were visited by a launch full of visitors who took the boys on the lake. One of the visitors put his thermometer into the water off the wharf; 72, thus they used the new wharf for the first time. Rev. Mr. Sprague and Mr. Clapp, from Shepard Hill, played ball with the boys, and stayed to tea. They were enthusiastic in praise of the Andrews Johnny Cake. As they were leaning and we were all on our sturdy new wharf suddenly we heard a cracking of timbers and the whole wharf fell in! No one was hurt, but many had their feet wet. We sang "Sun of my Soul", at prayers.

c. 1902

Chapter 10

August 6 - August 15

1893

By

William Woods

SUNDAY, AUGUST 6

AT 9 O'CLOCK ALL EXCEPT ANDREW, the Jewish and Roman Catholics boys, started off for church at Shepherd Hill. The Charlestown Choir boys sang with great effect. Mr. Sprague preached. The wind had breezed up while we were in church, and we hurried home, landing just before a smart shower came up. The boys went in swimming at Sandy Beach in the afternoon. Israel Bean had been taken with chronic disobedience during the day, and Thurston and I had long talks with him. He seems a good boy in many ways and says he is being taught by a lady on Beacon Street to be a painter. In the evening most of the boys read quietly, and at prayers they sang several rhymes. Richards relieved Whitney in the dormitory.

MONDAY, AUGUST 7

Thurston and Cutting went fishing at 4 A.M, and brought back some good perch. Benedict and Whitney left on the early train. The boys were rather grumpy about the outside work; especially those who had just came out of the kitchen. But Stanley and I took two boats full fishing and they were soon optimistic again. While we were out a shower came up, the first of a succession of showers, some with thunder and lightning, which lasted until 4 o'clock. Hailstones fell in one shower, and Jere Sullivan was much astonished to find that "them are made of ice in this weather." The boys behaved very well, reading, cutting birch bark canoes, and playing in the dormitory. At 4 o'clock they went swimming off the wharf, and after tea there were races in the White boats between the old and the new boys, the new winning. Andrew gave exhibition of the speed of an oarsmen.

TUESDAY, AUGUST 8

A splendid day followed yesterday's showers, and the departing boys seemed to look with envy on Jere Sullivan and Ernest Cameron, whom we have asked to stay another week. They both seem much in need of a little country life, and they are models of the deportment. Cutting took the boys down, and expected to have his hands full, as numerous fights were threatened, Israel Bean apparently being in all of them. The homesick Magnis went off having whined to go home all the week. Richards and one of the boys cruised around after our lost wharf, but did not find it. The faculty, ably led by the secretary, put in some good work of the new stone pier.

At four Stanley and I went to the landing to wait for the new boys and Mr. Cross They seem a rather good looking lot.

Stanley McMasters 11 years old   *39 Grove Street*
Robert Walker 15 year old   *25 Blossom Street*
Robert Kopp 11 years old   *11 Millard Street*
John Kopp 13 year old   *11 Millard Street*

Recent photo of Red Hill as viewed from the old Camp site. Thanks to conservation efforts, the view looks about the same as it did in 1893. However, Squam waters are now cleaner and healther than in the 1890's.

Walter Revell 13 years old	*442bl street, East Boston*
Robert Kissock 12 years old	*105 Lexington Street, East Boston*
Sidney Mckay 14 years old	*283 Lexington Street, East Boston*
Arthur Provost 13 years old	*191 Brooks Street*
Charles Smith 14 years old	*13 Dexter Street, South Boston*
James Renton 13 years old	*498 Swett Street.*

Told them something of the routine of the camp, assigned cots, and gave them a row before tea. We sang "From Greenland's Icy Mountains" at prayers. Cross thought it best to make an impression on the boys in the dormitory, so stood in an imposing attitude in the middle of the room until he heard a muffled "get on to the cop."

WEDNESDAY, AUGUST 9

Today has confirmed our first impression of the new boys, none of them has been homesick, and they have taken hold of the kitchen and dormitory work with the right spirit. Thurston, Cross, and Richards aided by numerous suggestion from Andrew, put up Major Gibb's flag pole in the morning, and after the dinner the flag was raised, to the tunes of "The Battle Cry of Freedom" and "My Country, Tis Of Thee." Thurston and Stanley went to Holderness in the afternoon, and all the rest of us played ball. Dr. O.M. Huntington called in the afternoon and asked the Faculty to call at his house. Boat races on the lake in the evening.

THURSDAY, AUGUST 10

The boys rowed on the lake after work was done, my crew being greatly excited by seeing a mink on the island opposite. As we were coming back the horn at the landing blew, and I went over and found Mr. and Mrs. Thayer waiting. They came over to the Camp, saluted on the way by some of the boys who were going around the island with our cheer "Rah, rah, rah –who are we - Groton School Camp 93." Are we in it- yes we are – Groton School Camp rah, rah, rah."

After inspecting the buildings they returned to Sleepers. Mr. Brass built a beautiful new letter box during the morning. After the dinner I took two crews fishing without startling success. "Uncle Willie" left for the Asquam House at five for an all evening junket at the Earnest Worker's Fair." He returned at one A.M. armed with a cane, a doll, and a box of candy. After tea we went for the mail, and Jere lost his hat and we captured a small turtle. Cross and Richards took two crews for a race around the island, going in opposite directions. Cross's crew, Issac, Johnson, Sidney, McKay and Bowman, won in 9:15. Richard's crew, Jim Renton, Ernest Cameron, Jere and Walker came in seconds later. Not a boy has been "on bounds" all day.

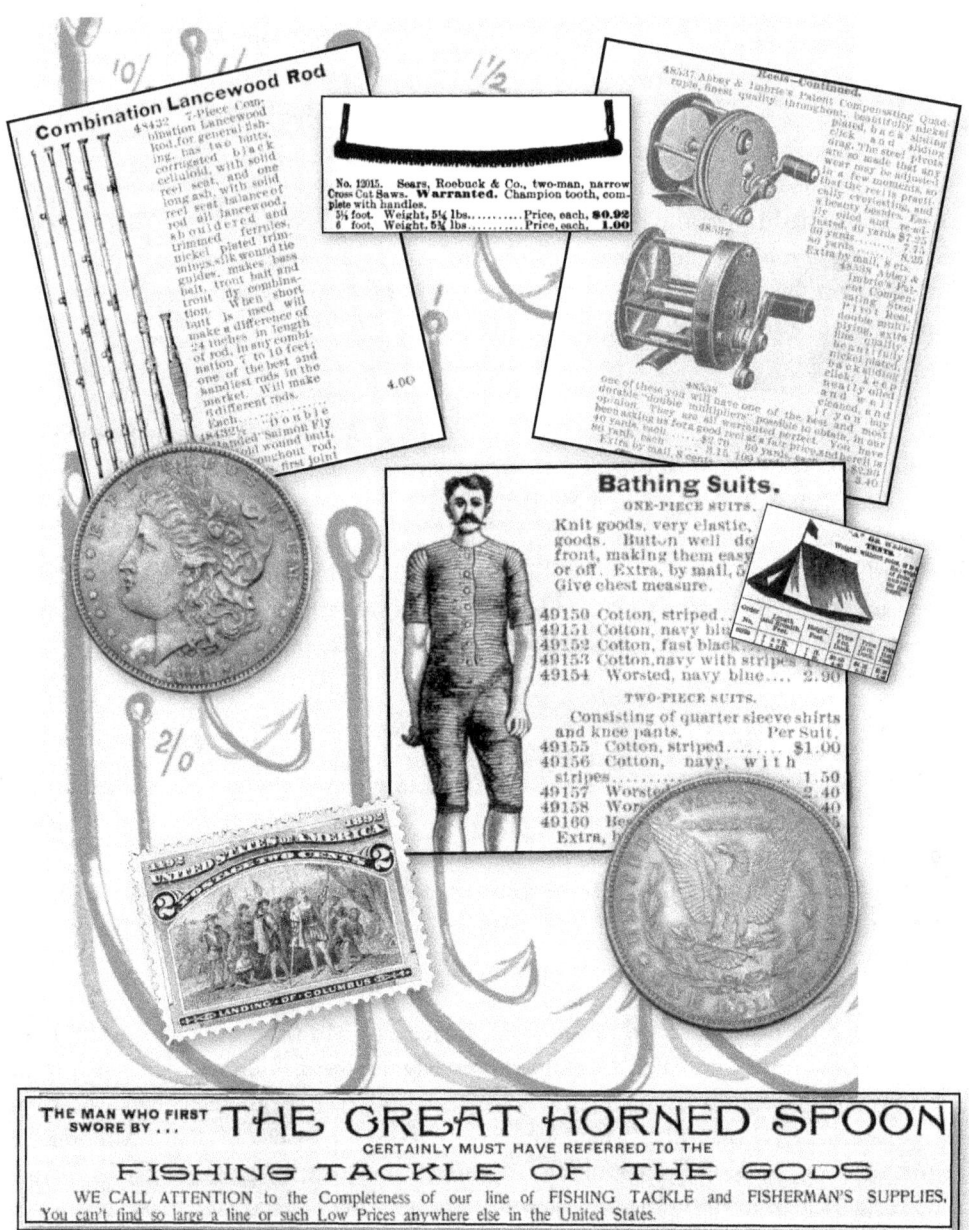

Images from the 1897 Montgomery Ward & Sears

FRIDAY AUGUST 11

Mr. Woods departs amid the tearful adieus of the assembled multitude accompanied by Mr. Thurston who goes to Ashland to escort his mother to the Asquam house. After work is over the boys indulge in some fishing, result—two small perch. We then go fishing with no result & we betake ourselves to Sandy beach and bathe. On our return Mr. Stanley, H.H.B, W.R.C. & Jeremy made improvements on the raft. Mr. Thayer arrives first before lunch but departs soon after to look after Mrs. Thayer's departure. H.N.R., W.R.C., Jeremy & Everest go over after ice and return with a big load. Andrew displays his strength by carrying a large blocks of ice up to the box. While we were gone, Walter Revell, Sidney McKay, Robert Walker, who had been allowed to fish in front of the camp undertook to row around the island for which they were put on bounds. Stanley McMasters, Bob Kissock and W.B.C. went after an extra supply of milk and returned to find T. P. T. had returned from his Ashland trip. H.H.R. gives Issacs, Johnson & Beebe punishment for not going out of the water when he told them to. They are not to be allowed to go in bathing tomorrow. 6:30 Mr. Thayer arrives & takes change. W.R.C.

SATURDAY, AUGUST 12

The early morning is spent in the usual occupations. After the regular work was done all hands set to work on the wharf. Larger "bricks" were imported in the boats and placed in position by the strong men. It is still an open question, whether Cross, Thurston or Andrew is the strongest man. They are careful to avoid a decisive competition. Good work was done on the wharf and it began to be serviceable. Cross then took the boys to Sandy for the morning swim. W.G.T. and Richards took Mrs. Thayer to Hotel Asquam to find more comfortable quarters for herself and family. They arrive a little late to dinner and hear the hungry Cross mildly express his opinion of them. After a boiled dinner, there seemed to be a general desire to play a game of ball. The weather looks threatening, but does not scare us. Cross and W.G. took the two boats ashore with all the boys except Theodore Thomford who has a lame knee. Two nines are chosen and one half an inning is played, when the weather carries out it's threat, with terrific lightning and torrents of rain. We seek temporary shelter under the trees but that failing us, the cry "to the boats" is obeyed with a rush. Everybody in a tremendous state of excitements and with great difficulty we get off from shore. Even the Yale captain is overcome and falls into the bottom of the boat, three times before reaching the Camp. The rain beats all former records and there is no longer any doubt in the boys minds that we "are in it". All clothes are changed and Jamaica ginger is administered under protests from Andrew, who objects to American coddling, and relates how he sailed for three weeks in a continued rain storm, without once changing his clothes. After supper there was a race around the island. Richard's crew; Issacs, Jere, Walker and Mckay. Stanley's crew; Cameron Johnson, Bowman, and Provost. Stanley won by 15 seconds. Time 8 min., 30 sec. breaking the record. After some rowing for pleasure, we had prayers, singing "Holy Holy Holy". Boys go to bed. Stanley comes in late with all the wet clothes which are dried over Andrew's stove. More protests and reminiscences.

Hotel Asquam

SUNDAY, AUGUST 13

A very beautiful day after a cold night. The weather had evidently changed. The Masters almost froze in the tents on account of the high winds during the night, but they are learning the art of keeping warm. W.G.T. was obliged to be away all day. He went to Ashland to preach in the morning and to Shepherd Hill in the afternoon. The Rev. Mr. Sprague had a sprained ankle and asked for assistance. The water was so rough that rowing to Church was impossible, so Morning Service was held in the dining room. Mr. Thuston read the Service and preached an excellent sermon, most acceptable to boys and masters. The boys spent the day quietly and were well behaved. They are an obedient crowd, and easily managed. The new boys give no trouble and punishments are exceedingly rare. After supper, a great many hymns were sung and prayers were read by Mr. Cross. Mr. Thayer's frequent blasts on the horn were not heard, because a strong wind was blowing in the other direction, and he waited an hour before he could get across to the camp. It seems as if a new landing place, nearer the camp would be a wise move.

MONDAY, AUGUST 14

A magnificent day—a little warmer and not a cloud in the sky. After breakfast and the regular work, all hands set to work outside. The wood pile was moved to a more suitable place, a little further from the dormitory and the place cleaned up. At Eleven o clock two boats started for Sandy's for a swim. The water was so cold, and the wind blew so hard that the boys stayed in the water, only a short time. Cross went for a sail in the light-boat and the boys sailed in the big boats, using coats and canvas, after dinner all, including Andrew, went ashore, leaving the camp to itself. We then climbed up past Sleepers and made the ascent of Mt. Livermore. N.S.T. and five boys went to the top; the others went to Round Hill just below the summit. The air was so clear that the views were magnificent. Richard and Cross released a captured swallow in one the of the deserted farm houses. The directing farmer, unfortunately, returned and charged fifty cents for broken glass. On the way down from the mountain, the boys picked blackberries and blueberries. The old squad filled tin cans and boxes to carry home. After supper there were two exciting races. Richards Crew, of the old boys were, Jere Sullivan, Cameron Isaacs and Sam Johnson. Cross's crew, new boys, were Mckay, Provost, Walker and Renton. The old boys won by a boats length, but there was some misunderstanding about the finish mark, so the race was rowed again, and the new boys won by quarter of a length. At prayers we sang several hymns.

THURSDAY, AUGUST 15

Cross left this morning with Richards and the boys. We hated to have them go. Cross stayed only one week, because his father was alone at home and looked for his company. The camp was more than sad to lose Jue Sullivan, who, tho not a thing of beauty has been a joy forever.

GROTON SCHOOL CAMP — 1893 JOURNAL

He is just the kind of boy for whom the Camp exists and whom it is calculated to help. Ernest Cameron is another good boy. Beeber, Gardner & Copitorn, did very well and Sam Johnson might have done better had he not been overawed by Fred Isaacs. The latter and Bowman, were I believe, unhealthy elements in the Camp. They were grumblers and generally disagreeable Isaacs confided to someone "that the camp was a rotten place and he wouldn't come again if he was asked". It is the opinion of the writer that he had better not be asked. After the old boys left, the boats brought back visitors. All the dwellers at Sleepers headed by Mrs. Thayer, came over and found us not in our tidiest trim. They stayed only a short time and returned to the shore. Little was done during the morning. The boys fished from the raft and rocks and a few went in for a swim.

At four o'clock Mr. Thurston & N.F.T. went ashore for the new boys. They arrived in great spirits at about five o'clock. One of them, Walter Farrer, 10 Wharf St. Chelsea, missed the train at Nashua, where he was to have joined the squad. They are from St. Stephens Church Boston, sent by the Rev. Mr. Torbett.

> *Andrew Campbell, 11 years, weight 72 lbs.*
> *281 West 5th St. South Boston .*
>
> *Cecil Hediard, 12 years weight 102 lbs.*
> *3 Rollins St. Boston*
>
> *James Fayer, 12 years weight 85 lbs.*
> *48 Reed St. Boston*
>
> *Charles Justin, 12 years weight 70 lbs.*
> *159 West 6th St. South Boston*
>
> *Frank Fouhs, 12 years weight 70 lbs.*
> *5 Conant Place, Roxbury*
>
> *Edward Demling, 13 years, weight 86 lbs.*
> *11 Longwood, Longwood*
>
> *Harold Oaks, 13 years, weight 99 lbs.*
> *14 State St. Cambridge*
>
> *Charles Fletcher, 16 years weight 115 lbs.*
> *33 Upton St. Boston*
>
> *Edward Hemonnier, 12 years weight 91 lbs.*
> *5 Garden St. Boston*

They seem to be an orderly crowd, but not particularly interesting. Two of them are old hands at camping. One of the boys has already had a week in the country and Charles Fletcher has camped out for nine successive years on Lake Winnipesauke! The writer would respectfully advise that in the coming years the lists should be carefully examined and revised, so that the Camp may be the greatest good to the greatest number.

With the boys came a gallant crowd of Masters: Charles Sturgis, Alfred Rodmen, William Howe and John Converse. They are most welcome and needful for our comfort and happiness. After the arrival of the new boys, we all went to Sandy for a swim. The water and wind were flatly cold, and only a short swim was permitted.

We returned for supplies, after which, Mr. Thurston took most of the new boys fishing and Rodman took the other boys for a row. At prayers, "All Hail the Power of Jesus Name."

On the Mainland

Above; a view of Squam from the Camp in 1893.

Chapter 11

August 16 - August 26

1893

By W.G.T.

MONDAY, AUGUST 16

THE NEW SQUADS WENT TO WORK after breakfast with excellent zeal. Rodman has the Dormitory; Sturgis, the Kitchen; Converse, the boats; Hare, the outside work. Hare and Converse put in the whole morning on the new wharf. They worked like beavers on the crib that is to serve for anchorage. The rest of the Camp were busy until half-past ten, in carrying stones to the wharf, and cleaning up on the shore to make a better landing for the boats. Arthur Provost was so much interested in the latter work that he hardly stopped for dinner and supper. Work done, most of the boys had their swim off the wharf and then many of them took turns in rowing. Mr. Thurston rowed down to the Asquam and brought back his mother to dine with us. Mrs. Thurston suggested that someone should fetch Mrs. Thayer. Rodman and Sturgis volunteered and returned successfully in half an hour. The two ladies seemed to enjoy the sight of camp life, and added materially to the delight of our day. After our guests had gone, we all went ashore for a ball game. Hare and Converse took a long walk to view the beauties of the surrounding country. Rodman and W.G.T. chose nines, and an exciting game followed. Rodman's nine won in four innings, score 11 to 10. The game was shortened by the unusually expressed desire for a swim. The boats were rowed to Sandy and the boys deposited. Hare and Converse preferred to go in from Sleeper's landing, but were interrupted by visitors. They waited, therefore, in places of shelter till help came and carried them to the Island, where they found good swimming from the raft. After supper there were several races by amateurs crews; time not taken. Andrew took his boys on the Lake after their work was done and made the evening melodious with "My Bonny", accompanied with an improvised trombone. The new boys sing well. The evening hymn was "Sun of my Soul."

THURSDAY, AUGUST 17

The weather looked threatening in the morning. After breakfast, Mr. Thurston, Sturgis and Hare worked on the new wharf. The plan for a crib was given up and stakes were driven in the sand, after John Copp had removed the larger stones and given an exhibition of his abilities as a diver. W.G.T. took a boat-load fishing, and Stanley, another, but the fish didn't seem to bite. Converse then took the boys to Sandy for their swim. The dark clouds did their worst after dinner, and it rained continuously all the afternoon. A ball game had been arranged for some of the boys, and a berrying expedition for the others, but of course all good plans had to be given up. Messrs. Sturgis, Rodman and Hare walked to Holderness in the rain, and caught a ride back with the groceries. The boys left at the camp amused themselves, as well as feasible and behaved very well considering the lack of entertainment. The punishments are almost unknown and discipline comparatively simple. The evening was spent indoors with casino, dominoes, go-bang, etc. till bed-time. We sang several hymns at prayers. "O Mother Dear, Jerusalem" and others.

GROTON SCHOOL CAMP — 1893 JOURNAL

The above campers would have been born between approx. 1881-83.

FRIDAY, AUGUST 18

A very cool night with incessant rain. The new masters were rather discouraged with the outlook, which is certainly discouraging for it still looks as if the sun were never going to shine again. The only incidents of the morning were attempts to fish between the showers and the usual swim from the wharf. In the afternoon Rodman and Sturgis took two boats for a row. More fishing and impromptu races. At five o'clock Mr. Thurston drilled the boys in the Dormitory. He taught them the ordinary marching movements, and several good exercises in the "development drill". The boys seemed to enjoy it all, and were in good trim for a second swim. Early in the afternoon, in response to the hour, Thurston went ashore and brought back with him the boy who was left behind on Tuesday. His name is Walter Farrar, 16 years old, Wght. 104 lbs., 10 Wharf Street, Chelsea. We find, on inquiry, that he has spent three weeks already in the country. His stay here will, therefore, increase his outing to five weeks. He seems to be strong and well, is as brown as a berry, and in no need of this extra fortnight. One cannot help regretting that the privileges of the camp are not always bestowed upon the most needy. The writer again urges that next year some remedy may be found. Three or four of the last ten boys have had from one to five weeks of country life this summer. Hare has had a bad cold all day, and has taken a new medicine every hour. At present writing he has survived his own doctoring. The weather did not permit the usual after-supper races, so the whole evening was spent indoors. The pent-up spirits of a rainy day were a little manifested at prayers. Three boys had to be talked to for misbehavior, but considering the long rainy day it was not a bad showing. The evening hymn was "My Faith Looks up to Thee".

SATURDAY, AUGUST 19

The morning dawned cool and cloudy. Some of the masters avoided the usual cool plunge. The master of the Dormitory has been conspicuously absent at that function since he came. After chores, Messrs Thurston and Hare went to work in earnest on the new wharf. By dinner time it was about completed, and the finishing touches were put on big Hare in the afternoon. It is a great success, and evident improvement to our comfort and good looks. The writer begs to record the credit deserved by Messrs. Thurston and Hare and their assistants for their efficient work and its manifested fruit. The boys spent the morning in the boats and had their swim at Sandy. The afternoon was spent in a most exciting ball-game. New boys against the old boys. The score after eight hard-fought innings had the familiar sound of 26 to 26. The weather during the afternoon was glorious, but towards evening the clouds began to gather. We had faith enough in the morrow, however, to send a message to some of the other camps inviting them to an afternoon service at Camp Chocorua. Sturgis and Rodman took the boys for their swim. In the evening there were races between two crews, coxswained by Hare and Converse. The former's crew consisted of McMasters, Fayen, Oakes, and Charmonnier. Converse's, of McKay, Revell, Smith and Walker. Converse won by a half-length. Messrs. Sturgis and Rodman visited Camp Chocorua, to ask for the use of the Chapel tomorrow afternoon. We

On the mainland to play ball

In 1893, the pitcher's mound was moved from 45 ft. to 60 ft.

Hugh Duffy batted .440

1893 Baseball Trivia

Having won the National League pennant in 1891, 1892 and 1893, there seemed to be no reason why the "Boston Beaneaters" would not pile up championships indefinitely. History tells us that, although they did not win the championship in 1894, they did do some mighty awesome hitting! Their hitting feats are impressive even by today's lofty standards.

sang "Rock of Ages", at prayers.

SUNDAY, AUGUST 20

Our "faith in the morrow" was misplaced. We awoke to hear the wind blowing a gale and the rain coming down handsomely. All plans for the services had to be given up to the great disappointment of all. The new masters are thoroughly depressed—they have had but one and a half fair days since they came. They are firmly convinced that the sun never shines on Squam. Sturgis is growing fat, for want of exercise and Hare, thin, for want of amusement. At half past ten Morning Prayer was said in the dining room. W.G.T. preached a short sermon. We sang, ""O Jesus, Thou art Standing", "Come My Soul, thou must be waking", and "The Sin of God goes forth to War." Two of the new boys were not present at the service. They did not hear the horn and professed ignorance of the fact that there was to be a service. They were put on bounds for culpable ignorance. After dinner, the great problem was what to do. A great many letters were written and all available books were secured. Still there were many unemployed. Two or three personal encounters were, therefore, not to be wondered at. John Kopp was especially warlike, and finally ran up against Hare. The latter won and Kopp is on bounds for all day tomorrow. Subsequently, he attacked Edward Demling and again found his match. The masters spelled one another in looking after the boys and supper-time was reached without further accident. During the afternoon, we had a call from Messrs. Holmes and Crane of Camp Chocorua. They sailed through the rain in Mr. Crane's canvas sloop, and sailed off with Sturgis. He returned later in the evening with large accounts of all he had eaten. The camp spent the evening in song. All the old favorites were sung and many so unfamiliar that the leader had difficulty in carrying the tune. The masters turned in early, with large hopes of fine weather tomorrow.

MONDAY, AUGUST 21

Worse and worse. The rain is harder than ever, the winds are howling and depression has reached low water mark. Hare wishes to see on record, that he protests. We have given up looking for the sun and are past the period of disappointment. Stanley and Hare started off at half-past nine, with six of the old boys, to get butter. They rowed down to the other end of the lake, and landed on some unknown shore. They attempted to reach their destination, but were lost in the woods. Stanley climbed a tall pine and by judicious shouting attracted the attention of a fisherman who guided them on their way. The butter seekers returned at about two o'clock, after a very exciting morning. Mr. Thurston drove to Ashland with Jim Renton, a good boy and one who ought to come again. To the surprise and delight of all, the sun in all his glory appeared just after dinner and he has been shining ever since. The afternoon was glorious and brought out all the pent up spirits of the camp. John Kopp became somewhat of a nuisance and at one time, during the rainy season, as threatening as the weather. Andrew administered a wholesome punishment, and, as a further punishment John was kept in the kitchen for the rest of the day. The usual Monday races took place in the afternoon. The

GROTON SCHOOL CAMP —— 1893 JOURNAL

Power Stroke

The winners.

old boys were: Renton, McKay, Walker and Provost, Coxswain, Mr. Rodman. The new boys, Farrar, Oakes, Chediard, and Hemonnier, Coxswain, Mr. Sturgis. The new boys won after a close and exciting race, by half a boat's length. The second crews, composed of the best rowers, not on the 1st crews, then had several races. The old boys won the first race, and divided the honors in the other races. We are very sorry to have the boys go away. The Journal has already recorded that they are an especially good lot, and with the exception of John Kopp and possibly McKay, might all be invited another year. They were all enthusiastic tonight, as they went to bed, and couldn't say enough of the good times they have had. At Prayers, we sang "Lead kindly Light". The writer begs leave to express his own appreciation of the camp and to record his thanks for a very happy ten days. W.G.T.

TUESDAY, AUGUST 22

A more than fine day. Rodman had much difficulty in keeping the dormitory quiet till the horn blew, as the prospect of going home was a little too much for some of the gents. After breakfast everyone loafed around waiting till it was time to go ashore. Hare in the meanwhile took some pictures. The boys left at 9 o'clock under the care of Rodman and Sturgis. Mr. Thayer went with them, as he was going to make a call on a "Lady Friend" of his in Sandwich. Her name is Hana, what a delicious time he must have had. Hare on coming back from the landing started immediately up the lake to go pay the old gent for his butter. Mr. Thurston and Converse aired all the blankets and beds; a good deal of a job. Mrs. Thurston came over to dinner which was a very good one. Andrew doing himself proud. At 4 o'clock Mr. Thurston and Converse went ashore for the new boys. Only nine came under the charges of Mr. Digby and Patten.

Fred McCarthy - 11 years   *356 8th St. - South Boston*
Wm. Lee - 10 years   *518 Dor. Ave. - South Boston*
Geo. A. Deans - 12 years   *134 W. 9th St. - South Boston*
Edward Morrill - 14 years   *96 7 St. - South Boston*
Wm. Mills - 13 years   *502 Summer St. - East Boston*
Harry Mills - 15 years   *502 Summer St. - East Boston*
Geo. Williams - 14 years   *218 Everett St. - East Boston*
Leonard Taylor - 10 years   *47 Lawson St. - East Boston*
Charles Maclane - 15 years   *128 Webster St. - East Boston*

Some of the boys are very large and some very small. They don't seem to have been able to strike a happy medium. After the arrival they went over to Sandy for a swim. In the evening Mr. Thurston, Patten, Hare and Converse went to a ball at the Mt. Livermore House, coming home from which Hare and Converse met with a mishap. The camp in the meantime had

GROTON SCHOOL CAMP — 1893 JOURNAL

Pinic at Squaw Cove

Mount Livermore House

some visitors. H.C.C.

WEDNESDAY, AUGUST 23
A perfect summer day. The faculty (some of them) took a dip at 6:30 A.M. After breakfast the usual camp work was performed under the direction of Patten; Dining-room & dorms, Hare. Outside work, Converse. The new boys seem fairly intractable and not indisposed to behave. At 10:30 all went in for a swim. E.H.H. took one load of juniors to Sandy Beach, and afterwards for a row around the island, gathering a lot of pond-lilies. Mr. Thurston went ashore to take some letters for Mr. Thayer to take out. At 1 o'clock dinner, very sumptuous, tomato soup, roast beef, and pudding. In the afternoon, Mr. Thurston went with Andrew and two boys to Mt. Livermore Hotel for a call. Patten, Hare, and the senior master took the others ashore for a ball game. The game was characterized by much grumbling, disputing, kicking and a few physical conflicts. Cecil, one of the captains, refused to play owing to his disapproval of the umpire. A good many others were conspicuous for sulking. After the game, at 5 P.M. another swim was taken. There was some fine diving off the dock and the float led by Patten. At six o'clock, while at supper, sounds of a horn were heard from shore and Stanley went over with two or three boys, returning shortly afterward with Richard Wheatland, a welcome addition to the faculty. He was assigned for duty as superintendent of boats, docks and flag. The "mishap" referred to by the writer of yesterday's annals should, for the sake of historical accuracy, be described somewhat in detail. The two gentlemen concerned in it had withdrawn quite early from the ball and were walking homeward in an apparently pensive mood, probably disappointed at the lack of social attractions, (or was it their lack of social attractiveness!) at the ball field. In this mood, Converse suggested that it would be soothing to sit down and gaze for awhile at the moon. A smooth fence-rail at the roadside presented an inviting appearance and he deposited himself thereon where he was soon joined by his companion. The rail was extended across a brook which flowed in a rocky gully at some distance beneath. But the added weight of Billy Hare proved too great a strain on the rail which suddenly broke midway, letting its occupants fall some six feet into the water and onto the rocks beneath. Fortunately no bones were broken and they returned quite bruised and wet to camp, having added something to their knowledge of the strength of materials and to their disgust at social festivities for campers.

To return to Wed. 23rd, prayers at 8:15. "Am I a Soldier of the Cross" was sung, and then the boys went to bed. Later Wheatland and Patten rowed to Chocorua Camp, but found their friends there absent and returned shortly. Played casino, Wheatland and E.H.H. against Thurston and Andrew. The former won two games, and then Andrew's side "played the rubber" game which they won. All to bed at 10:30.

THURSDAY, AUG. 24
A north wind increasing in force, and bringing rain about 10 A.M., promised a cold disagreeable

The Whitehall Rowing Boat

Some hold that the Whitehall rowing boat design was introduced from England. However the famed nautical historian Howard I. Chappelle, cites the opinion of the late W. P. Stephens that in New York City there is a Whitehall Street and this was where the Whitehall was first built. Chapelle, Stephens and others agree that the design came into existence some time in the 1820's in New York City, having first been built by navy yard apprentices who had derived their model to some extent from the old naval gig.

Quoting for "Rudder" magazine, August 1943, Captain Charlton L. Smith states a somewhat contrary view, "This delver into nautical lore has never been able to ascertain whether the Whitehall boat originated at Whitehall, New York, or at Whitehall, England. It is extremely likely from the latter place. At any rate the model of a "pure breed" Whitehall that was so useful a rowed-on-the gunnel workboat at Boston and at The Battery at New York City and, later, at San Francisco, evolved from the English Wherry."

The first documented race in American rowing history, as reported in Gaine's New York Mercury of April 26, 1756, took place between a New York City crew and a whaleboat traveling from Cape Cod to Albany. The first international boat race was also held in New York Harbor. A British frigate, Hussar, arrived in New York Harbor in 1824. Its captain, George Harris, was a fan of rowing and had brought with him a crew and a boat that had raced on the Thames. Hearing of the Whitehall boatmen and their competitions, he challenged them to a race and offered the winner a $1000 prize. The race attracted great interest throughout the city. On the day of the race, as reported in New York Evening Post, "the concourse of spectators that assembled on the Battery and lined the wharves of the North River to witness the race was immense, not less than 50,000...The victors rowed immediately round Castle Garden to Whitehall where the boat was hoisted up...a band of music all the time playing Yankee Doodle." (Dec. 9, 1824). The crowd drawn to the river was all the more impressive because it represented a third of the entire population of the city at that time.

It was after these early beginnings that rowing began to gain in popularity throughout the rest of the country. The races between the Whitehall crews attracted the interest of some Yale undergraduate students. They traveled to New York to buy one of the boats used by the Whitehall ferrymen and thereby introduced collegiate rowing to America.

http://www.whitehallrow.com

day. After breakfast and morning work, Wheatland and Patten put up the sail in the "Lady of the Nashua" and went out sailing taking a few of the boys, who could swim, successively for short tacks back and forth in the narrows. After an hour the rain became violent and forced all to the shelter of tents and the house. The storm lasted through the whole day. In-door amusements were the only admissible ones. The brethren preserved a commendable cheerfulness. Hare and Patten grooved out a drain about the floor of the faculty tent which checked mainly the inflow of rain. The platform on which the tents are pitched is a memorial of the energy and architectural skill of its constructors. But, in the opinion of the writer, it is much too high. Its designers evidently had a fear of toads and snakes or other nocturnal disturbers. But a visit from a snake or toad is rare in any camp and not to be especially dreaded. But the great elevation of the tent platforms, while very agreeable in fine weather, exposes them to the wind in cold and stormy weather and the rain beats in rivers and torrents flooding the floors during a driving storm. One foot from the ground would be ample elevation in my opinion. Patten and Wheatland went to Camp Chocorua for tea. At prayers sang "O Paradise."

FRIDAY, AUGUST 25
The weather cleared during the night and a glorious day was the result. After the usual morning with a large squad of volunteers was put at work filling the space under the dock and around the posts with stones. As this labor was in a way a preliminary swimming exercise, it was very popular. At 10:30, regular swimming was taken up, with the usual enthusiasm. Dinner at 12:30. Green corn and beef steak. After dinner went ashore for baseball. The old boys played the new boys. Wheatland and Patten played with the New, Thurston and Converse with the Old. It was a good game without the squabbling and kicking of the previous one. Score 16 - 16. A home run by Wheatland, and a phenomenal, back-handed, running catch by Thurston were the features of the game. After the game another swim was taken. After tea there was some miscellaneous singing by the youngsters, who have mostly good voices. Then a party, under Hare and Stanley, went out fishing, returning in an hour with an eel and a number of bull-fish. Prayers at 8:15. Hymns, "Children of the Heavenly King", and "Abide with me," After the youngsters were put to bed the attractions of the splendid evening, with the full moon gleaming on the water, drew the faculty out on the lake in the boats. During the lovely boat ride E.H.H. lost the ruder of one of the white boats. Called at Camp Chocorua, and found no-one at home. But later met these campers just returning to their camp. Returned to Groton School Camp at 10:30 and to bed at 11:00.

SATURDAY, AUG. 26
Another beautiful morning greeted our eyes. The morning work was prolonged by some extra scrubbing and cleaning of floors. The dining room and dormitory were washed and well polished off. Then for an hour the youths were kept at work putting sand upon the paths.

Faculty tents

Swimming at 10:30. Dinner at 12:30. After dinner a party was organized for black-berrying and climbing hills. Wheatland and Hare took about a dozen lads ashore. Have started for the summit of the hill back of Sleepers with five or six boys, but all but one of the little ones gave out before reaching the top. Have reported a fine view of the lake, the islands and the surrounding heights. The berry-pickers were very successful, bringing in over twelve quarts. Meanwhile another party under Converse and Andrews went for berries to another point and obtained four or five quarts. The berries were a popular addition to supper which consisted, beside them, of warm biscuit (seventy-five were consumed), bull-fish, mush and doughnuts. In the morning a supposed loon was discovered showing its black head as it swam along some hundred yards from camp. Wheatland had brought a rifle and he proposed to shoot the bird. Several fine shots were made by him, Patten and Thurston, but the bird was not hit, and to their surprise it neither dove nor rose in the air. Later investigation showed it to be a floating shoe. Patten and Wheatland went to Camp Asquam for tea. The oil supply had given out and no lantern could be displayed from the flag-staff. Prayers at 8:15. Hymn, "Onward Christian Soldiers".

Typical 1890's Sears Wagon at $39.90
(Approx. $1037.00 in 2007 dollars)

Pepsi is Born. In 1893, Caleb Bradham, a young pharmacist from New Bern, North Carolina, begins experimenting with many different soft drink concoctions. Like many pharmacists at the turn of the century he had a soda fountain in his drugstore, where he served his customers refreshing drinks, that he created himself. His most popular beverage was something he called "Brad's drink" made of carbonated water, sugar, vanilla, rare oils, pepsin and cola nuts.

Also in 1893, the zipper was invented and displayed at the Chicago Worlds Fair. The only customer was the Postal Service. They used them for mail bags.—

GROTON SCHOOL CAMP — 1893 JOURNAL

Same spot—then & now—in front of the old playhouse.

Popular Ditty In 1893

Song
The Cat Came Back
1893

Written By: Harry S. Miller (with later folk additions)

Old Mister Johnson had troubles of his own
He had a yellow cat which wouldn't leave its home;
He tried and he tried to give the cat away,
He gave it to a man goin' far, far away.

But the cat came back the very next day,
The cat came back, we thought he was a goner
But the cat came back; it just couldn't stay away.
Away, away, yea, yea, yea

The man around the corner swore he'd kill the cat on sight,
He loaded up his shotgun with nails and dynamite;
He waited and he waited for the cat to come around,
Ninety seven pieces of the man is all they found.

But the cat came back the very next day,
The cat came back, we thought he was a goner
But the cat came back; it just couldn't stay away.
Away, away, yea, yea, yea ....

*Also in 1893, the "Birthday Song" tune was written by Mildred Hill and her sister Patti.

Chapter 12

August 27 - September 5

1893

1= Camp Algonquin   3= Camp Chocorua   5= Asquam House
2= <u>Groton School Camp</u>   4= Mooney's Point   6= Camp Asquam

SUNDAY, AUGUST 27

THE MORNING WAS CLOUDY and lowering causing fear of rain. The rain did not come however and the whole camp set out 9 o'clock in four boats (Sleepers "glide" having been secured) for church at Shepherd Hill near the Asquam House. Rev. Mr. Sprague preached from the text in Judges "Curse ye Merad saith the Angel of the Lord." Curse bitterly for he came not up to the help of the Lord against the mighty." The boys behaved well. Returning we reached the camp at 1:30 while at dinner it began to rain, a shower with some thunder, lasting for an hour. These boys are a very docile and easily managed around. James Fayen has been homesick and weeps often, and there are other reasons why he might be well omitted from next years list. The afternoon passed quietly after tea a member of hymns were sung prayers at 8:15. Patten had a toothache for which many remedies were prescribed by those who thought themselves wise in medicaments, including tobacco, famacia ginger and landascum. The treatment was only moderately successful.

MONDAY, AUGUST 28

The morning looked dubious in regard to another, but finally evolved a fair warm day. After morning work Hare and Stanley went with a party for ice. Several boys were put on bounds by Converse for making disturbance in the dormitory A target was erected on the opposite shore and several of the faculty did some shooting at it with Wheatland's' rifle. It was too remote (over 100 yds.) to perceive which shots took effect. But on going over to it there were discovered two hits out off ten balls fired. Dr. Huntington of Harvard College called about noon and invited the camp to an entertainment at Chocorua on Wed. eve. After dinner Wheatland and Hare took five boys on an expedition to climb Red Hill at the head of the lake. They returned about 5 o'clock, having made the ascent and having succeeded in getting all the boys but one to the top with them. These boys who live mainly in the city streets when at home have but little staying power with their legs, and such tramps on the surrounding hills are a useful discipline for them. After tea the boat race between the old and new boys occurred. The crews were: old boys, Farmer, Oaks, Lemonier and Leland. Coxwain W. Hare. New boys were: H. Mills, W. Mills, McLane and Morrill, Coxwain W. Patten. The old boys won by about a boats length. The new boys then raced a second crew of old boys consisting of Justin, Demling, and Fayen. The new boys lost this race also, being out of breath and somewhat broken up by their first race. The Hymn at evening prayers was "Jesus lover of my soul."

TUESDAY, AUGUST 29

The sky was heavily clouded over when we rose, and before breakfast was over it began to rain with increasing violence. The event of the morning was the departure of the old boys under charge of W. Hare who had, unfortunately, bad weather for the last days of his camp service as had been the case during very much of his stay. The youngsters were fitted out by the faculty and Andrew with out-side garments to protect them from the rain till they reached the railroad and all put off in good spirits in spite of the storm. The rain continued throughout all the day

GROTON SCHOOL CAMP — 1893 JOURNAL

Races on the mainland

T.K. Brown & P. Stone in boat

and the was passed in recording and games, even swimming was omitted. About four P.M. Thurston,, Wheatland, Stanley and Converse went to Sleeper's landing and soon after returned bringing J.W. Alsop and the ten new boys. The old boys greeted them from the dock with the camp cheer which in its present form goes as follows

'Rah, rah , rah ! Who are we?
Groton School camp, ninety- three!
Are we in it? Yes we are!
Groton School Camp, rah-rah-rah'!

Have sent back report of the weight of the out-going boys who (all but Justis) showed a gain of from two to seven pounds, Justice having increased by the latter figure.
The new boys are:

William O Neil 12 yrs.	*3 Sudbury Place, Roxbury*
Frank Wright 13 yrs.	*9 Duncan St.*
James Hermitage 14 yrs	*3 Faunce Place*
Fred Hermitage 12 yrs	*3 Faunce Place*
John Kitson 19 yrs	*1 Sherwood court*
Albert Gibbs 14 yrs	*24 Weston St.*
Frank wood 13 yrs	*1267 Tremont St.*
George Reed 12 yrs	*2 Dunlow Place, Roxbury.*
Robert Thompson 13 yrs	*3 Sherwood Court, Roxbury*
Albert Pidgeon 15 yrs	*1299 Fremont St.*

WEDNESDAY, AUG 30

The weather cleared during the night and some complaints of discomfort from the cold were heard in the morning. A lovely clear day made all happy. After morning work and some hard labor was expended in scooping out gravel from the side of the dock and putting it in the walks and filling in and grading the same—a work which can be continued indefinitely with useful results. Swimming at 10:30. In the afternoon, Wheatland and E.H.H. took four boys and made the ascent of the Rattlesnake Hills. The boys went up without a murmur and in good time. A fine view of Lake Winnipesauke was obtained, and also of Mt. Chocorua. The other boys went ashore and played ball—the Old versus the New. Patten played with the Old and also with the New. Since 28 to 21 in favor of the new. Thurston began making shutters for the house windows with view for the final closing up. In the evening the whole round went to camp Chocorua in response to Dr. Huntington's invitation. Dr. & Mrs. Huntington and the ladies of his party, Balch, Wiggin and Thorndike devoted themselves to the entertainment of the boys with great facility and enthusiasm, and fed them lavishly with ice cream cake and lemonade. At 8:30 P.M. we left with grateful appreciation of the hospitality of our hosts and

GROTON SCHOOL CAMP — 1893 JOURNAL

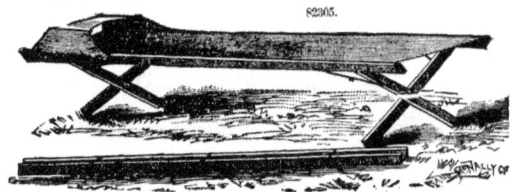

THE "U. S." FOLDING COT.

No. 82305. The "U. S." Folding Cot. Just the thing for camping purposes Covered with either white or brown 10 oz. duck. This is the lightest, strongest and most compact folding cot made. It has the only practical pillow ever put on a cot. It is easier opened and closed and folds into less

Faculty unwinding

returned to camp and after prayers all went to bed.

THURSDAY AUGUST 31

The day was clear cool and lovely. After the usual morning routine of work the scooping out of gravel was resumed and some good work done resulting in much improvement in the paths and landing place. At 9:30 A.M. Richard Wheatland and H. C. Converse took their leave of camp A sloop constructed for them by Alsop, Andrew and Thurston went ashore and finally Alsop took out a boat for fishing, then the horn sounded at the landing. Patten went over and lo:

> *Alberta Secoct Allen*
> *Margaret Almira Smith*
> *Rebecca Garham Allen*
> *Ammie Louise*
> *Maroin Boyd Allen*
> *Mabel Montgomory Bease*
> *Charlotte Blemset Barrell*

The seven ladies above recorded and one other appeared at the landing and requested to be allowed to visit the camp. Patten had gone over supposing that Andrew or Thurston were at the landing and his costume was somewhat more scanty than that in which he is want to shine in female society, consisting at this time a sort of compromise between Highland Hills and bathing suit. But he boldly accepted the situation and brought the ladies over in two trips. They made a visit of half an hour, inspecting the tents and dormitory and expressing much pleasure at our arrangements when they left. Alsop was summoned in and was induced with some difficulty to lay aside his difference and assist in transporting the ladies on their return. After tea some practice in boat racing was conducted by Alsop and Thurston in which the old-boy crew had the advantage. Patten was visited by some gentleman from Camp Asquam. Prayers at 8 o'clock. Hymn, "The Church's One Foundation."

SATURDAY SEPT 2

A dull cloudy and chilly morning foreboded rain, which began to fall at 11:o'clock. A general cleaning up of camp and grounds was undertaken by all hands. Thurston completed work on the window-shuttters. Andrew went off to Squam Bridge before breakfast after supplies, returning at 9:30. He has prepared the meal before he left and it was brought on by the boys under direction of Thurston. After dinner some exciting races were held between the sloop yachts "Billy Lee," Stanley designer and "The Peezar" constructed by Alsop. The Billy Lee proved to be the faster boat in a strong wind, which prevailed at the time. The weather became clear about noon and after the races we went ashore for baseball. A very exciting game was played by nines headed by Patten and Alsop. The former won, score 47 to 45 just before the

Camp—c. timeless

game a telegram arrived announcing the death of the mother of the Hermitage boys, and they were taken by Thurston at once to Ashland to reach the train for Boston. Rev. F.B. Allen and his two daughters came onto the ball-ground and witnessed the closing part of the game. Two home runs by Alop and some very difficult catches by Patten deserve to be recorded. Albert Pidgen showed good abilities as a ball-player. Thurston at 7:o'clock having succeeded in getting the Hermitage boys on the express train for Boston. He brought with him, to the delight of the camp, Messers S.W. and Ned Sturgis. The boys were gathered for prayers at 8: o'clock. Hymn, "All Hail the Power of Jesus Name."

SUNDAY, SEPT 3
The morning was clear and cool. The faculty, including the new arrivals, all took the matutinal plunge. After breakfast all started for church at Shepherd's Hill. The party went in four boats. Rev. Mr. Woods preached from the text "Or Every One Of Us Must Give An Account Of Himself To God." The boys behaved well. It was the birthday of Frank Wright, who now is to be recorded as 14 years of age. After dinner all went ashore for a walk. We climbed the ridge back of Sleeper's. Mr. Sturgis and Alsop went on to the wooded Summit to the right of the ridge. A fine view of the lake and the mountains was obtained. Mr. Salbert and Farnham from Camp Asquam came to tea, and remained till after prayers numerous hymns were sung. After the boys were put to bed, Andrew made some pancakes which were served for the faculty supper. After this the gentleman from Asquam sailed off for their camp. A light rain was falling.

MONDAY, SEPT 4
A clear, cool, lovely day. The principal morning work was the general washing of towels. Stanley worked moving stones for a breakwater and to strengthen the dock. The Messers Stugis went for a call to Chocorua. After dinner all went ashore for a ball game. An interesting game was played between nines headed by Patten and Alsop. Alsop's side won score 24 to 21 after this game the weekly Boat races were held. The old boys with Patten for coxwain were H. Mills W. Mills and Morrill and McLane.. The new boys coxwained by Alsop were Pidgeon, Thompson, Gibbs and Wright. The race was interrupted after the first start by the breaking of an oar. A new start was made by about one length. A race between the seasoned crews of old and new boys was then held. Williams, Dean, Lee and McCarthy were the old boys. Woods, Kitson, Read and O. Neil, the new boys, won by one length. In the morning of this day the camp was visited by Rev. Mr. Allen and three daughters, also by Mr. Balch. The latter gentleman remained to dinner and various suggestion about the development and management of the camp. After dinner he [Balch] amused the boys by letting them shoot his revolver at a target offering a prize of a pound of candy to the one who would hit it. No one was successful. Prayers at 8.o.clock. "Hymn, Oft in Danger, Oft in Woe." After prayers the faculty rowed over the Chocorua for the scow, with which to take off the bedding and other furniture to Chocorua to store for the

We may live without Art, we may live without Books
But Groton Camp boys cannot live without Cooks.

winter. The scow was found with water in it and it was decided that bailing it would take too long, so they returned without it. With this day the records of the writer come to an end, who testifies to his great enjoyment of and faith in Groton School Camp and pleased by the great efficiency, fidelity and enthusiasm of all his assistants, to whom he records his gratitude.

SUNDAY SEPT 5
A bright morning and the excitement of the move kept up the spirits of the boys. Having washed their towels, and loaded their bags with apples (many are obliged to carry their clothes over their arms) the youngsters gathered for the final instructions. They were simple; after a search about the clearing, with chairs in the dining room, dormitory and tents, we ended at the flag pole where all sang from Gibbs, the Patride songs. Half an hour later Messers. Sheraton, and Sturgis sorrowfully watched the wagons depart and returned to the stand to put things in order for Winter. All movables were stored in "Eighty-One" at Camp Chocorua. The Chocorua members fairly outdid themselves in their hospitality during the next two days. By Wednesday night the work was finished, and our camp deserted.

End of the first Season of Groton School Camp 1893

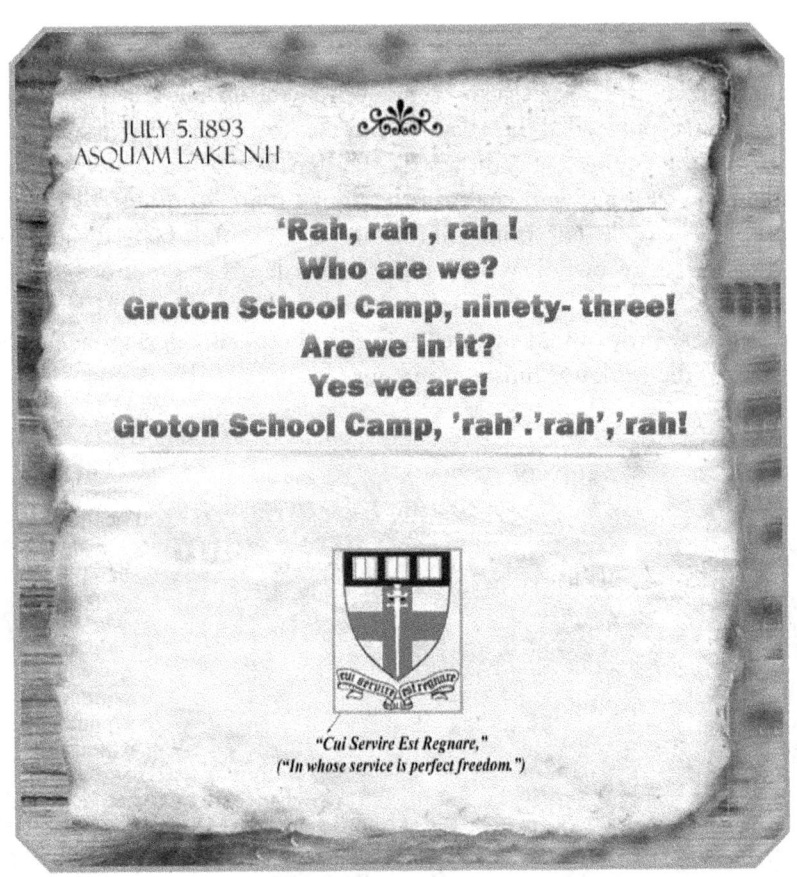

Aₙᴅ ꜱᴏ ᴇɴᴅᴇᴛʜ ᴛʜᴇ ꜰɪʀꜱᴛ ɢʀᴏᴛᴏɴ ꜱᴄʜᴏᴏʟ ᴄᴀᴍᴘ ꜱᴇꜱꜱɪᴏɴ ᴏꜰ 1893. The Camp continued on Asquam (Squam) Lake until 1920. The nearby Webster family bought the Island in exchange for the larger Mayhew Island on Newfound Lake—with enough money left over to build the necessary structures.

—Every true lover of nature who has come into close touch with Newfound and her immediate surroundings is laden with sweet memories. In the midst of his toil, he remembers the solitary quiet he enjoyed beneath the whispering pines of Belle isle, completely cut off, as it were, from his fellow men; he remembers that romantic little voyage up the shady windings of Fowler's river; he remembers the enchanting views he obtained from the summit of Mayhew island, from Grove hill, or from Bear mountain— but the one thing which has left the most vivid picture in his mind is Sugar Loaf and the Ledge. In its total impression, Sugar Loaf is truly great and sublime.[1]—

Sleepers Farm, Bristol NH c.1904

---

[1] *History of the Town of Bristol, by R.W. Musgrove 1904*

Part V

Newfound Lake Era
1920-1966

—Meat loaf was made with 25 pounds of hamburg, a case of Campbell's vegetable soup and 4 loaves of stale bread—
                    Sam Chauncey

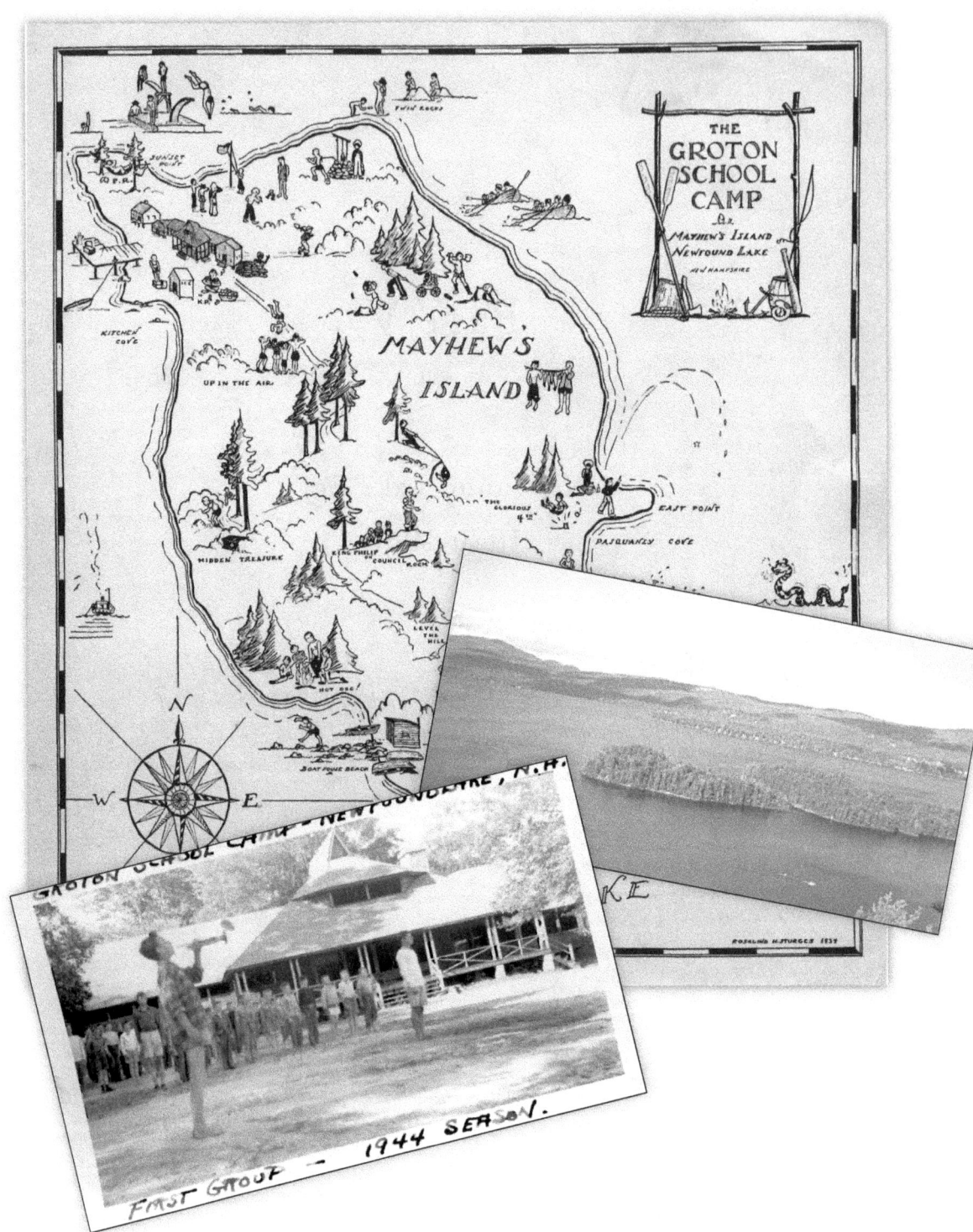

Chapter 13

Groton School Camp, Mayhew Island
Newfound Lake NH
1920-1966

The move from Squam Lake to Newfound Lake in 1920 required new facilities to be built. E.P. (on right) —with Brethren—taking a tea break from their inspection visit.

c. 1920

This building burned down in 1990 and was replaced.

c. 1920

Linc; rear row center

Storing ice

Kitchen crew on their way to serve at GSC. (1937)—Dykie in center.

Linc at left rear

GROTON SCHOOL CAMP — Newfound Lake Era—1920-1966

Linc on right 1st row.

We do not wish to dwell on the difficulties of running the Camp or give a list of needed repairs or wages or food costs. These are our problems. We do urge you to look at the picture again and think that this is the end-product of the Groton School Camp — underprivileged boys with a chance to enjoy themselves in the country.

Please think that your contribution will be put to efficient use to provide the barest necessities and simplest pleasures for the boys on their visit. They will enjoy their stay to the utmost and will greatly appreciate what you have given them.

GROTON SCHOOL CAMP COMMITTEE

Donald White   Henry Chauncey jr.   David Olyphant

Howard B. Corning   John Huston Finley III

1953

P.S. Remember that contributions are deductible for income tax purposes.

1947

To Those Interested in the Welfare of the Groton School Camp
A STATEMENT — AN EXPLANATION — AND AN APPEAL

After careful consideration, the Trustees of the Groton School Camp have decided not to open the Camp this summer, in order that the entire year's income may be devoted to long overdue repairs and replacements to the Camp plant. The budget on which we operate is so slim that in any given year we can afford to operate the Camp or to undertake capital improvements, but not to do both.

The list of present needs is formidable. The ice house must be wholly rebuilt or replaced by a new refrigeration plant; the Faculty Shack must be entirely reshingled; two porches are unsafe and must be replanked; the superstructure of the float needs renewal. Most important of all, however (and most expensive!) is the necessity for the complete modernization of our primitive sanitary facilities. The State Inspector is obviously dissatisfied with our present arrangements, and feels that improvement is essential.

Fortunately, owing to the high rate of employment throughout the districts from which our boys are recruited, there is less than the usual need for free camp facilities for teen age boys. The social service agencies advise that, if we must suspend operations, this is the year when the loss of our services will be less keenly felt than at most times. The high cost of food and other operating expenses, the recent death of our chef, the fact that Howard Lincoln ("Linky") has spent twenty-four consecutive summers at the Camp and deserves a sabbatical—all these are additional reasons for closing now.

We regret the loss of continuity of service of an institution which we sincerely believe is doing a worth-while job, but feel that we must suspend operations at this time if we are to be of greater usefulness later. In order that the job of repairing the Camp plant may be adequately financed, we urge very strongly that you, nearly all of whom have been faithful friends of the Camp, repeat at this time your normal subscription.

JOHN CROCKER	ACOSTA NICHOLS, JR.
HOWARD A. LINCOLN	R. MINTURN SEDGWICK
FRANCIS P. NASH, JR.	CHARLES H. STOCKTON

Trustees of the Groton School Camp

Back kitchen porch area before refrigeration—ice was stored instead.

Lower step with jacket; Fred Hertack (cook)

Linc looking out from front of Fac Shac

GROTON SCHOOL CAMP — Newfound Lake Era—1920-1966

Linc on right

GROTON SCHOOL CAMP —— Newfound Lake Era—1920-1966

GROTON SCHOOL CAMP —— Newfound Lake Era—1920-1966

Back of Fac Shack

"Ham" Richards, and Gary Studds

GROTON SCHOOL CAMP — SEASON OF 1941		
Receipts		
Bal. in Ayer Bank, Oct. 31, 1940..	$1041.70	
Bal. in Bristol Bank, Oct. 31, 1940.	201.41	
	$1243.11	
Athletic Exchange	175.00	
Sale of Christmas Cards	69.17	
Scudder, Stevens & Clark Fund	645.00	
Groton-St. Mark's Dance	871.57	
Book Store	400.00	
Graduates and friends	1667.60	
Registration Fees	635.49	
Sale of Candy at Camp	169.79	
Refund from Railroad Co.	103.60	
New York Big Brother Movement	64.70	
	$4801.92	
		$4801.92
		1243.11
TOTAL		$6045.03
Expenditures		
Food and Milk	$1460.15	
Salaries and fares for staff	999.79	
Shingling Main Roof	710.20	
Ice	116.00	
Printing Christmas Cards	47.10	
Printing and mailing appeal	64.79	
Laundry	66.07	
Transportation (train and bus)	420.35	
Fire insurance	186.00	
Liability and workmen's compensation insurance	104.28	
Refund of registration fees	126.00	
Drugs and medicine	25.60	
Candy for store	120.33	
500 pine and spruce seedlings	6.40	
Painting and repairs to boats	100.00	
Johnson (boat delivery and special services)	40.00	
Hospital (scarlet fever case)	79.25	
Doctor	112.92	
Supplies	90.34	
Plumber	12.76	
Garage	45.73	
Miscellaneous expenditures	158.03	
	$5092.09	

GROTON SCHOOL CAMP — Newfound Lake Era—1920-1966

GROTON SCHOOL CAMP — Newfound Lake Era—1920-1966

Sam Chauncey 1956

Shake Hands & say goodnight

Booma Lacka, Booma Lacka
Bow Wow Wow
Chica Lacka, Chica Lacka
Chow Chow Chow
Razzle Dazzle
Ice to The Ice Tines
The Reds, The Reds
Yeah!

Howard Lincoln, Camp Director, By Sam Chauncey 4/06

Howard Lincoln was a giant of a man.

While the Groton School Camp, which he ran, was a small program, his influence in the lives of those who were connected with GSC was enormous.

Linc, as he was called, spent his entire life in education. He taught in school and college during the regular academic year and he "taught" on Mayhew Island in the summers. He was associated in one way or another with Groton School Camp for more than thirty years.

Linc and Florrie, his wonderful wife, and their son David, in his early years, lived in the small cabin at the south end of the island. Each morning about 6:30, Linc would ride up to the north end in his boat (with it's one and one-half horse power engine puttering along), carrying a small, metal milk can. (This he filled from the Camp's refrigerator and brought back with him at night). He spent the full day at the Camp, and while he and Florrie had dinner together in their cabin, Linc often came back for "Faculty Supper" when the campers had gone to sleep.

Linc did everything. He was the Director; he was the medical man; he was the mechanic; he was the disciplinarian; he kept the books and he was the ambassador to the east shore of the lake and to Bristol.

Linc had an extraordinary sense of humor. At Faculty Supper, with the staff sitting around a table in the dining room by the light of a Coleman lantern, eating peanut butter and jelly sandwiches, we would turn on the one radio in the Camp. If the Red Sox were on, we listened to them and Linc had a running patter about each player. On nights when the Sox were not playing we would listen to "Bob and Ray" or "This is Your FBI". Linc should have been a writer for both programs for he had comments, quips and interspersed lines which had us in stitches.

He ran the Camp on a shoe string. I recall that the budget for our final year was about $10,500. Meat loaf was made with 25 pounds of hamburg, a case of Campbell's vegetable soup and 4 loaves of stale bread; an engine was rebuilt dozens of times; every paint brush was washed and dried after use, so to be used again. And watching him negotiate with local stores and shops makes today's investment bankers look like amateurs.

As a person, Linc had three extraordinary qualities. First, he understood everyone he met. He took a little time to take stock and see what the person was like. But once he understood him, he had a habit of finding something the person was good at and then encouraging him in that effort. He built people up. Second, as a disciplinarian he was tough, but he was always fair. While he had favorites among the boys and the staff, if you made a mistake Linc told you directly what it was, he explained why it was wrong and he set the penalty. You came away knowing what had happened and understanding why you had been disciplined. Third, he saw everyone on the basis of their own intrinsic merit. He had the interesting situation of dealing with a number of Groton Students and faculty who came, often, from wealth on the one hand; and he dealt with youngsters from south Boston and New York's Bronx on the other. He saw nothing but each person's strengths and, if by chance, the person had none he tried to find an area the person could be strong in. But for the lazy, whether they were rich or poor, he had distain and he was tough. We all love rewards and Linc was a master at giving them out. He trained me to fix things and repair equipment around the Camp. One night at Faculty Supper he appeared with a framed, hand-drawn certificate which indicated that I was a "master" in repairs at GSC. word memorial was liberally used for the living, not the dead.

Down in the lower right hand corner, in very small type he had written "But not for refrigeration equipment" as I had almost ruined the engine that cooled our ice box! If you worked hard on a project, the result was named for you – The Chauncey Memorial Path, for example– the This wonderfully generous, firm, kind man was the heart and soul of Groton School Camp. He made it "tick" and he gave to each person who came on the island a sense of self-worth that helped each be better person later.

Linc in front of hurricane hut (1950's)

"Little Linc" On Mayhew Island, 1934-1948
By David Lincoln 2008

When I was three, my Dad was in his 4th year as Director of Groton School Camp on Mayhew's Island. A photograph, taken on the back porch of the Faculty Shack, captures my first visit to the Island. It was after the Boys had gone home, and my Dad brought my Mother and I up for a few days, sleeping in the back room, aka "infirmary" of the Faculty Shack.

Dave with parents Florrie & Howard

Fast forward 4 years, 1936, when "Bull Bull" (F.P.) Nash, a Master (mathematics) at Groton School and Camp Manager, authorized building of "Linc's Cottage" down near South Point. From this time on, my Mother Florrie and I spent each summer on the Island. In this delightful location I spent the next 12 summers ensconced in my own room, (complete with double deck bunks and a day bed, and/ or in the attic, when numerous relatives came to visit.

Life was simple but complete, kerosene lanterns, wood and kerosene cook stove, cooking water pumped from the lake, and the "only $75 outhouse in the State of New Hampshire." My chores included daily trips to Camp for 2 quarts of fresh milk and bi-weekly trips with glass gallon jugs for drinking water at the well pump by the playroom ball field. The latter trips were usually made by row boat—euphemistically referred to as "Dave's Boat", a 14 ft. Swampscott dory.

Being an only child on a island may seem to be a lonesome life—but I had plenty to do; whittling soft pine into boats etc; bandaging the cuts which were part of the learning process; foraging for berries in season for Florrie's pies and muffins; entertaining my cousins; splitting kindling for the stove and fireplace; and potting a few red squirrels with my Dad's trusty 22. (Red squirrels can turn a cottage into swiss cheese if left undisturbed for the winter),

Little linc on Peaked Hill

Naturally the lure of those 48 campers at the other end of the Island was all consuming, so when I turned 10 I was allowed one, two week period to be a "Junior".. and the following year a "Senior", participating in all the activities from Work Squads to Prayers. Possibly due to my station in Island life, (but I would like to think due to ability alone), I received a Red (GSC monogram) letter as a "Junior" and Black as a "Senior" camper.".

Getting the Camp ready and putting it to bed were time consuming tasks for Linc the director, and as I grew older and stronger I was the #1 (and only helper putting in the pumps and the pipes for water, cleaning out the five Camp boats and "Dave's", putting the raft and docks in and away, and shuttering the buildings . (Honesty forces me to admit that the Grotties who stayed after Camp, did their part, but the two Lincs had more than enough to keep busy) .

So—life was good !! At 15 I started to play on the Bristol Town Baseball team. I was bringing home trout from the Newfound River several mornings a week, and turn

Dave (Little Linc) in his boat with Spot.

ing into a real teen-ager. Unfortunately, this was not to last.

Big Linc, in cahoots with my Uncle, got me a job at a fish camp so far up in Vermont that I had to take French lessons just to get there. "Dave", my Father said, "you are just too big for your britches around the Island, and I think a change of scenery would serve us all well".

So off I went to Quimby's in Averill, Vermont, for the next three (delightful) summers—Camp prospered and I prospered in the ways of the world—nothing untoward you understand, just self-sufficiency and confidence. And before and after Quimby's I still played some ball and helped with the pre and post Camp stuff.

My interaction with the Camp had several facets, the campers in my two years of participating and the camp counselor Grotties—several of whom became quite famous, George Lodge, Fred Quinn, Chub Peabody, to name just a few. (At one point I was the proud owner of a Groton School, black and white striped football jersey someone left behind).

And of course Linc's reference to a variety of counselors, boys and kitchen kids provided me with the Director's insight into the foibles of one and all.

It doesn't seem that this was happening 75 years ago—it is all so fresh in my mind's eye. But—that's the way fond memories should be !!!

The mission—*yes*— I believe the mission was met, more so in some cases than others as one might expect. Witness the dedication of Sam Chauncey and Jack Richard's among many other "privileged" who got and maintained the message (the letters of appreciation at the dedication of Lincoln House came from many of the Grotties who had the Island experience)—not to mention Jack Crocker who followed Rev. Endicot at Groton.

Look at the dedication of so many "campers" who have followed the program, and contributed to your efforts *[this book]*. *I don't think we will ever know the totality of what lives were changed*—but I do know of the many kids who came to visit Linc and Florrie through the years, with their thanks evident in their approach.

I would never have had the appreciation for Linc that I have were it not for those summers on the Island, and the subsequent Groton and other honors that came his way because of his sincere contribution to the "underprivileged". After all, he was one himself, growing up in Somerville's "brick bottom" district. If his brother Frank (10 years older) hadn't been active in the Diocese and as a camp director himself, Linc would not have followed the path he did, and contributed to so many lives.

Dave Lincoln Oct. 2008

Leveling the ball field with Howard's new cart.

Father & Son—Linc and Little Linc.

Linc's Cabin 1930's

Clockwise from top left, Howard Lincoln with son David, interior of Linc's cabin, Linc with son David, Linc playing the "flute".

Linc's Cabin (note: as of 2008, Linc's Cabin still stands)

GROTON SCHOOL CAMP — Newfound Lake Era—1920-1966

Mayhew Program Recalls Its Origins

By BEA LEWIS
Staff Writer

BRISTOL — The past and the future connected Saturday, at Mayhew Island on Newfound Lake, when ceremonies marking the centennial of the founding of the Groton School Camp were held.

The 55-acre island, the largest on Newfound, has been home to the Mayhew Program for 25 years. It is an offshoot of the Groton School Camp founded on Squam Lake in 1893.

An Episcopal affiliated charity camp, Groton offered poor inner city youths from Boston and New York a chance to learn the skills they needed to avoid becoming delinquent. In 1921, the camp moved from Squam to Newfound Lake. It closed in 1966. Two years later, the Mayhew Program was established.

Although it is no longer church affiliated, the Mayhew Program
MAYHEW, Page 6

David Lincoln, the son of Howard 'Link' Lincoln, who ran the Groton School Camp for half a century, hand-painted a number of wall plaques to recreate those lost when the main lodge on Mayhew Island burned in 1990. They were unveiled during a centennial celebration held Saturday.
(Citizen Photo/Bea Lewis)

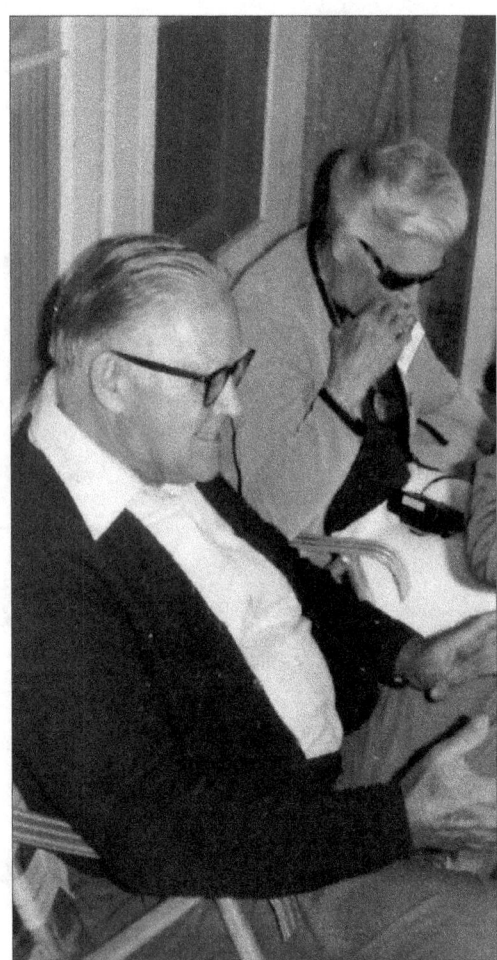

Top; Little Linc at Mayhew dedicating new GSC team plaques. Bottom; Linc and Florrie.

GROTON SCHOOL CAMP
BRISTOL, NEW HAMPSHIRE

1957

1957

Staff

    Studds -- director
    Richards - Asst. director
    Finley - ath. director
    Polk - " " (juniors)

Openers:
C.P.R., Chauncey, Studds, Richards, Finley, Kitchen Crew (except Riddle), Polk, Busk, Pike, Simmons, and Crosby

First Period:
Ashton Crosby, Hardwick Simmons, Jake Cooley

Second Period:
Hardwick Simmons, William Kemble, William Niles, John Weekes, Charles Brinley, Joseph Frelinghuysen

Third Period:
Nathaniel Coolidge, Wallace Dailey, Edward Lawrence, Daniel Pierson

Kitchen Crew

    James Chase -- cook
    Douglas Dyke -- asst.
    Ray Riddle -- Pots
    Herbert McLucas - Storeroom - Dining Room
    Kenneth Chisholm - Dishes
    Hugh Ellis - Dishes
    Robert Scott - Dishes

Henry (Sam) Chauncey (1956 director) was on hand for opening and closing and for the first period. The writer greatly appreciates his interest in the camp and his assistance.

                                    Howard A. Lincoln

                                    Permanent Resident

Paul Abry, Camp Director, By Bill Polk, 2006

A favorite Groton School Camp picture is of Paul Abry and Sam Chauncey sitting on the porch of what was at the time the new house for the director: the two wise men of Mayhew Island at ease before supper discussing the day's events, or the lovely view of the Mountains, or perhaps even what movie sound track would boom across the lake after dark from the motel resort on the mainland.

A teacher and minister at Groton School from 1942 until his death in 1968, and director of the Groton School Camp during the 1950's and 60's, Paul once told me that he was not a great teacher or a powerhouse coach; his real usefulness to the school was as an advisor to students and as the head of the dorm for new students, where he could help them deal with homesickness and adjust to the demands of Groton. He understood that for most kids the journey from youth to adulthood was not a straight line. Bumps on the road could be unsettling, if not devastating and detours could lead to a sense of being lost. When bumps and detours occurred, Paul was always there holding up a road map with directions back to the main road. I remember a student with a volatile temper that would cause him all sorts of trouble. Paul got a hold of him and told him to come to his study whenever he felt himself "losing it." The student would spend an hour or so behind closed doors venting. Paul would listen, offering a word here or there, and when the storm had past send the student nack to his work or play. Paul brought the qualities of empathy, care, and wisdom to his work as director of the camp. Be it a homesick camper or a kitchen crew's or counselor's problem, he was there, part father figure, part friend, with a discerning ear, and understanding word, and a reassuring smile. There is one other talent Paul brought to the camp. I can't recall the name of his softball team, but I do remember how he could hit a softball if he got his pitch, inside belt-high. At bat, he would let a few pitches go by, teasing the pitcher, " A little higher, please." Or " Make the next one a little more inside." If the pitcher did, boom, Paul would hit the ball over the roof! As director of the Groton School Camp, Paul hit lots of home runs, most of them by the way in which he influenced campers, members of the kitchen staff, and counselors.

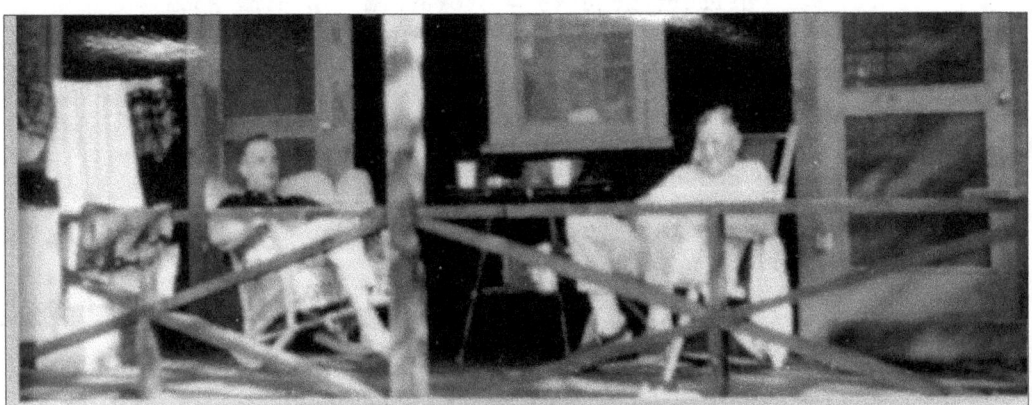

Sam Chauncey and Paul Abry relaxing.

GROTON SCHOOL CAMP —— Newfound Lake Era—1920-1966

Charlie Bundy, standing

Camp (USCG) boat, bought at auction in Eastham Mass.

David Auchincloss Bill Polk Paul Abry

Back porch kitchen. White gas, pull start refrigeration motor/compressor on left.

GROTON SCHOOL CAMP — Newfound Lake Era—1920-1966

Phil Tilney

Bill Polk

Henley Bros. pumping kitchen waste up hill.

E. Hall

3rd row; George Butler, Jon Choate, (?) Bob Devens. 2nd row; David Auchincloss, Buzz Hall, Bill Devens, Harry Pollock, Paul Abry. 1st row; Bill Polk, Sam Chauncey, Em Hall, Sarge Cheever.

2nd row; David Auchincloss, Bill Sloan, Sarge Cheever, Jon Choate. 1st row; Em Hall, Bill Polk, Ed Rogers, Charlie Brinley

1959 kitchen crew; Back L-R, ?, Bob Scott, Tom Gregory, ? Front L-R Hugh Eilis, Doug Dyke, Herbert McLucas, Chip Chisholm

1956 kitchen crew; Back L-R Doug Dyke, Jack McDonald, Bill Evans, Jim Chase. Front L-R Ray Riddle, Ken "Chip" Chisholm, "Butch" Herbert McLucas

2nd row; Harry Pollock, Charlie Brinley, David Auchincloss.. 1st row; Bill Polk, Paul Abry, Ed Rogers.

John Paterson

Caulking Junior Boat c. 1939

Paul Abry at the helm. Sam Chauncey at Starboard.

Bill Polk diving

Chip giving haircut

1959 kitchen crew; Top Doug Dyke Bottom L-R Bob Scott, Herbert McLucas, Hugh Eilis

L-R; Hugh Ellis, Tom Gregory, Doug Dyke, Jim Chisolm

Top; Hugh Ellis, Bottom; Doug Dyke, Center L-R ?, Butch McLucas, Arnie Kaup, Bob Chase.

GROTON SCHOOL CAMP — Newfound Lake Era—1920-1966

Top L-R ; McLucas, Jim Chase, Bill Evans, Jack McDonald. Bottom; L-R Doug Dyke, Ray Riddle, Corky

Left: Ass't Cook Bob Evans. Right: Head Cook Jack McDonald

Al McLean 1955

Serious stuff—carving initials in the lodge's front porch.

L-R; Jim Chase, Doug Dyke, Ray Riddle

Ken Chisolm

Hugh Ellis & Ken Chisolm

Ye Olde Lodge

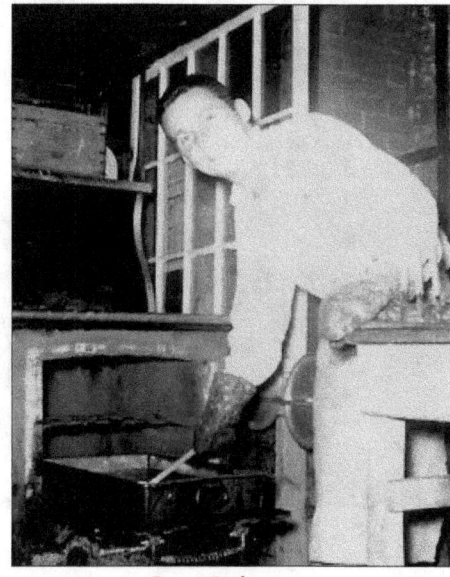
Doug Dyke

Doug Dyke

Above, Kitchen Crew 1962; L-R- Jeff Manson, (K.Harmon), (K.Bingham), (M. Lincoln), (McLucas), (J. Lincoln), (Donnie Harmon)

S. Cheever & Sam Chauncey

L-R; Charlie Brinley, Ed Rogers, (?) Paul Abry, Sam Chauncey

Paul Abry

Rev. Murray Kenney, Christ Church Cambridge Ma.

Tom McNeally

Harry Pollock *Ed Rogers*

Paul Abry

Sam Chauncey's Recipe 1956— "Meat loaf was made with 25 pounds of hamburg, a case of Campbell's vegetable soup and 4 loaves of stale bread.. ("Proof of the pudding" shown above.)

"Nature, People, and Spirit" *A Tribute to the Groton School Camp, 1893-1966*

Though the modern Mayhew Program began in 1969, its roots go back much further, to the founding of the Groton School Camp in July of 1893. Inspired by the Rev. Endicott Peabody, the legendary founder and first headmaster of the Groton School, the Groton School Camp was one of the earliest charity camps in America, working with disadvantaged boys from the Boston and New York areas.

Above Left: Attendees join the boys for a Mayhew Island lunch. Above Right: Master of Ceremonies for the day's event, the Reverend W. Murray Kenney.

Still blowing the Mayhew Island bugle: W. Murray Kenney in 1935 (above left) and 1993 (above right).

An August 7th Groton School Camp Centennial Celebration attracted more than three dozen representatives of the old G.S.C., from Geoffrey Swift, a camper in 1923-24, to staff members from the 1950s and 1960s, many of whom later played a role in the establishment of the Mayhew Program. At a commemorative service, Jack Richards and Sam Chauncey, both of whom were Groton School Camp counselors and founding trustees of Mayhew, stressed the continuity of Mayhew Island as a special place for helping children in need. Chauncey quoted his grandfather, himself the director of the Groton School Camp in 1895, who defined "environment" as three things: "nature, people, and spirit." It was that combination of factors that made Mayhew Island so special in the past, noted Chauncey, and which continues to make it so special today.

The celebration was both respectful and light-hearted. The Rev. W. Murray Kenney, who first arrived on Mayhew Island as a bugler in 1930, served as a memorable master of ceremonies, whether leading a raucous singing of 1930s Mayhew Island songs or playing taps on an old battered bugle. David Lincoln, who grew up on Mayhew Island as the son of longtime director Howard A. Lincoln, unveiled a commemorative wall he and Mayhew staff member David Long had created, much of which recreated old G.S.C. plaques lost in the great lodge fire of 1990.

Many of the returning G.S.C. friends would agree with one attendee, who described the celebration as "one of the most memorable days in my life." The celebration meanwhile helped the boys and staff of today's Mayhew view themselves in a new light, as part of a long history of work on Mayhew Island. "It's humbling," one Mayhew staff member commented, "to know that we put in our year or two or even ten at Mayhew, but that people have been here working toward a similar end for a hundred years. You also realize that we owe it to all those people never to give anything but our best for the kids."

Chatting with today's Mayhew boys: Walter Brent (G.S.C. camper '39) and Tudor Richards (counselor '35).

GROTON SCHOOL CAMP — Newfound Lake Era—1920-1966

Sam Chauncey addresses the boys and visitors.

Top and Above Left: The Groton School Camp Commemorative Wall: Restoring plaques destroyed by fire; reconnecting to Mayhew Island's past. Above Right: Catching up on the last sixty years: Winthrop Lee and W. Murray Kinney.

A 1993 Mayhew boy visits the Groton School Camp exhibit.

Still a special place: Former Groton School Camp counselors and boys, together again.

Groton School Camp - Season of 1962

HAVE you ever walked through the city streets on a hot summer's day and seen the heat rising in waves from the asphalt? It's rough! Have you ever seen the kids "swimming" in the Frog Pond on the Common? It's crowded, not too clean, but better than nothing. Can you imagine the face of one of these kids lighting up if he were told he could have two weeks on an island in a New Hampshire lake? You can help make that imagined look of happiness a reality. GROTON SCHOOL CAMP has the island, has the staff to look after the kids, and a small part of the necessary funds to operate, but only your help, your contributions, will make the opening of the camp this summer a sure thing.

We need about $8400 to function for three two-week periods. A $30 contribution takes care of one boy for one week. And this only takes care of the essentials. It doesn't provide for improvements, replacing worn out equipment, or any luxuries. This summer we are going to have to replace the kitchen stove — cost about $500. We are still on the lookout for some boat replacements, and we need them badly — cost unknown but high.

We know you are called upon to help a lot of organizations — most of them very worthy. We too must call on you; we feel we are equally worthy. GROTON SCHOOL CAMP provides two weeks in a clean healthy setting for a large number of boys from Greater Boston. It also provides a rewarding experience for some Groton boys as they work with underprivileged kids. Both grow in this relationship.

We are financed in some measure by the School Missionary Society, and in some measure by income from the School bookstore and athletic store. But the bulk of our financing must come, as it has in the past, from the graduates and friends of the School. We hope you will want to share again in this enterprise — in fact we are counting on this as we make our plans for this summer.

THE GROTON SCHOOL CAMP COMMITTEE

The author, top far right

GROTON SCHOOL CAMP —— Newfound Lake Era—1920-1966

Mr. and Mrs. Lee Ambler
William Amory
Francis I. Amory, Jr.
Arthur and Catherine Armitage
David Auchincloss
J. Howland Auchincloss, Jr., MD
Richard Baker, Jr.
Harold Heeder
Kenneth and Patricia Bingham
Mrs. Jonathan Bingham
Thomas A. Bingham
Standish Bradford, Jr.
John M. Bradley
Walter Brent
Charles E. Brinley II
William Bundy
George Butler
Martha and John Chandler
Charles M. Chapin III
M. Chapin Krech
Sam Chauncey
Kenneth and Maryanne Chisholm
Jonathan Choate
Grenville Clark III
Stuart H. Clement, Jr.
Mark M. Collins
Mr. and Mrs. Warren Cook
James C. Cooley III
Hamilton Coolidge
Lawrence Coolidge
Nathaniel S. Coolidge
Roger S. Coolidge
John Crocker
Letty Elise Crosby
H. Ashton Crosby, Jr.
Philbrook S. Cushing
John S.F. Daly
James S. Davison
Daniel deMenocal
Charles Devens
David Devens
Lithgow Devens
Richard Devens
Tyson Dines III
A. Webster Dougherty, Jr.
The Honorable Clive DuVal
Douglas and Patricia Dyke
Edna Dyke
Malcolm J. Edgerton, Jr.
Kenneth and Doris Eldredge
William Evans
David H. Fairburn
Oliver D. Filley, Jr.
Alexander Finley
John H. Finley III
Alexander Forbes
Christopher and Elizabeth Forste
Hamilton Forster
Reginald Foster III
Maxwell E. Foster, Jr.
Richard Fox

William B. Frothingham, Jr.
Harrison Gardner, Jr.
Priscilla Gemmill
George Putnam
John Glessner
Ward Goodenough
Shippen Goodhue
George and Joan Gordon
Marshall Green
Richard and Margot Grosvenor
Arthur Hadden
Harold F. Hadden
Edward H. Harding
A. Brooks Harlow, Jr.
Fletcher Harper
Norman Harrower Jr.
Eliot Hawkins
James J. Higginson
Betsy Hopkins
Eleanor and Cleon Hopkins
Susan and David Hopkins
Richard Hopkins
William Hoppin
Marshall Hornblower
John Howard
David and Mary B. Howe
Coleman W. Hoyt
Michael Humphreys, MD
Michael Huxley
Hugh M. Hyde
Stephen B. Ives, Jr.
Oliver B. James, Jr.
Theodore G. Kane
Edmund H. Kellogg
Bartow Kelly
William T. Kemble, Jr.
Murray Kenney
Edith Keppel
Jonathan Ketchum
John M. Kingsley, Jr.
Hugh Knowlton
Eleanor Knox
Philip B. Kunhardt, Jr.
William E. Ladd II
Francis C. Lawrance
Edward P. Lawrence
William Lawrence
James Lawrence
Lewis R. Lawrence
Richard H. Lawrence
Richard Lawrence
John T. Lawrence, Jr.
Richard G. Leahy
Winthrop and Barbara Lee
David and Jean Lincoln
Stuart W. Little
George C. Lodge
William Caleb Loring
Michael Luther
Huntington Lyman
Frederick J. Mali

Mrs. Nathan Marvin
Dan Mathews
William Mavel
George K. McClelland
James F. McClelland, Jr.
Alan McIlhenny
J. Alan McLean
Nancy McManus
John W. McNealy II
Joseph Messina
Thomas N. Metcalf, Jr.
John A. Morgan
Ann Muhlebach
Michael H. Murray
Peter Nash
Peter Nitze
Alexander Northrop
David and Elizabeth Noyes
D.K. O'Conner
David Olyphant
Dick Ostberg
William Paine
John D. Peabody
Malcolm E. Peabody, Jr.
Daniel H. Pierson
Henry Pierson
Alan J. Pifer
William Polk
Fletcher J. Pomeroy, MD
Henry Porter
Peter and Kathryn Powers
Charles Putnam
Eben Pyne
Percy Pyne
Cynthia Rawle
Christopher & Elisabeth Richards
Edith Richards
Francis and Amy Richards
Joanne and Hamilton Richards
Jack and Wendy Richards
Tudor and Barbara Richards
Elaine and Raymond Riddle
George L. Rives
Donald and Elizabeth Rowell
Thomas W. Rush
Paul S. Russell, MD
Kent Sanger
David A. Schroeder
Robert L. Scott
Sarah D. and Robert T.
Richard S. Scott, Jr.
Anthony T. Sears
James R. Sheffield
Hardwick Simmons
William P. Simons II
Lee T. Smith, Jr.
Edward Stevens
Charles Stockton
Bayard Storey
James Storey
The Hon. Gerry E. Studds

John Suter
John Sweetser, III
Robert Taft
Arthur J. Tallis
Cortlandt M. Taylor
Mike Thomas
William Thompson
David and Rose Thorne
Robert W. Tilney, Jr., MD
Howard Townsend
Reverend Joseph Tucker
Samuel A. Tucker
Frank Van Ummersen
William G. Van Pelt
Chuck Van Ummersen
Lincoln Van Ummersen
Mr. Lou VanUmmerson
Eugene Wadsworth
George H. Walker III
Joseph Walker, Jr.
William B. Warren
Bradford Washburn
Louis C. Washburn
David P. H. Watson
Walter and Mary Watson
Richard H. Webb
John M. Weekes
Eugenia West
Donald White
Edgar P. E. White
Jean and Frank H. White
Richardson White, Jr.
Edward Whitney
The Rev. and Mrs. John Williams
Donald R. Williams, Jr.
Nicholas Witte
The Reverend John Woolverton
George L. Wrenn
Roger Larochelle
Alfred H. Hopp
Elizabeth Valentine
Betsy Hopkins

L-R: GSC Alums Ken Bingham, Dave Howe and Sam Chauncey meet up at Mayhew 5/06 for a "Booma Lacka" cheer. *(2006- Not 1906!)*

Above, some of the names, supporters, and co-authors to this history.

Endicott Peabody U.S. Educator (1857-1944)

EARLY IN THE AFTERNOON on November 17th, 1944, Mr. Peabody' offered to drive Mrs. Acland to the station in Ayer, Mass. She noticed he had a little trouble with the foot pedals of the car and so made some pleasantry about it. As they drove, Mr. Peabody remarked "Franklin Roosevelt is a very religious man." These proved to be his last words. A few hundred yards later, just after they had descended the hill, one-quarter of a mile beyond the old golf course now disused, Mr. Peabody slowed the car, drove to the side of the road and turned off the ignition. He slumped in his side, Mrs. Acland looked at him and to her amazement saw that he had certainly fainted and appeared dead. She went immediately to the house owned by Mr. Arthur Havemeyer, less than one hundred yards away, and sought help.

Mr. Peabody was dead. To those who knew him, the manner of his death seemed symbolic; a mercifully swift departure accompanied by a massive final act of will for the sake of another, an act accomplished at the very instant of death.

The Chapel Service was unforgettable. Graduates, parents, trustees, friends, neighbors, fellow headmasters, and many who had not known, but admired, him came from near and far; New Yorkers by a special train. It seemed a triumphant occasion, with sorrow tempered by pride and affectionate gratitude. Mrs. Peabody died peacefully in 1946.

Endicott & Fannie on Squam—1940

Franklin Delano Roosevelt said of Peabody, "As long as I live his influence will mean more to me than that of any other people next to my father and mother." (As quoted in Peabody's obituary in the New York Times, April 13, 1944.) —

R<small>EMEMBER</small>! Things in life will not always run smoothly. Sometimes we will be rising toward the heights—then all will seem to reverse itself and start downward. The great fact to remember is that the trend of civilization itself is forever upward, that a line drawn through the middle of the peaks and the valleys of the centuries always has an upward trend. — "Cui Servire Est Regnare" —E.P.

Endicott Peabody

Amazingly, the old playhouse structure still stands—thanks to the efforts of the nearby Webster Family.

1893

Part VI

The Current Program

—The Mayhew Program—

—Success is a result of working hard and learning from challenging experiences.—

Mayhew Island, Newfound Lake N.H.

Chapter 14

The Mayhew Program

1969—Present

THE MAYHEW PHILOSOPHY
SOME THINGS WE HOLD TRUE...

- *Success is a result of working hard and learning from challenging experiences*

- *Individuals learn to make good decisions when given encouragement and clear expectations.*

- *Personal growth is inspired by people who are trusted, respected, and who abide by the same standards they profess.*

- *Having a sense of belonging promotes creative thinking, responsible behavior, and the courage to try.*

- *Everyone can contribute to the community.*

The Mayhew Program History

MAYHEW'S ROOTS GO BACK TO 1893, when the Groton School, a private boarding school in Groton, Massachusetts began operation of a summer camp for underprivileged boys on Groton Island in nearby Squam Lake. It was the first charity camp of its type in the country.

In 1920, with the help of the Webster family, the Groton School Camp was moved to Mayhew's Island, an uninhabited island used for sheep grazing and lumber. The GSC served needy boys from New England's urban areas until 1966, when the focus of Groton's efforts turned to matters on campus.

A few years later, with the island buildings falling into disarray, several former GSC counselors joined forces with the staff and trustees of nearby Camp Pasquaney to begin the Mayhew Island Project in 1969, serving 9 boys from the inner city neighborhoods of Manchester, NH. Jonathan Choate, a Groton teacher—with the able assistance of key staff like Owen Lindsay, Jr, a Pasquaney alum—supplied the leadership that first year in what was the only summer-long session in our history.

Tony Governanti, a Tilton School teacher recruited by our patron saint, Owen S. Lindsay, was hired as director the following year to expand "Camp Mayhew" by serving more boys from throughout New Hampshire.

In 1974, Mayhew incorporated as the "Mayhew Program" and began its work as a year-round program. By the late '70s, enrollment was at 72 boys. Al Cantor, a staff member during 1975 and 1976, succeeded Tony in 1984. Within a few more years, enrollment in the traditional program was consistently at 84 boys annually.

A pivotal day and point in the history of Mayhew was on January 6, 1990 when the Owen Lindsay Lodge burned to the ground on a blustery winter day. The outpouring of support was phenomenal. By the following June, a new lodge was built despite the 6 weeks of unsafe ice and the logistical quagmires of getting all the materials and workers out to the island in time to open camp that summer. Symbolic of the program's dealing with challenge was when Owen Lindsay received the phone call informing him of the disaster even while the fire was still blazing, Owen calmly asked, "what do we need to do to rebuild for the upcoming summer?"

Mayhew has been blessed with great leadership at all levels over the years. Together, we continue to improve the program and make the refinements that keep us fresh and strong. Every year, new individuals bring ideas and improvements to the program. One of the most major program changes was the development of the Link-Up pro-

With Groton School's Jon Choate leading the way—Mayhew Is Off And Running
(Edited News Story Below)

MANCHESTER (N. H.) UNION LEADER — Tuesday, July 8, 1969

9 Model City Youngsters Get First Taste of Camp

THE FIRST PROJECT under the Model City Agency became a reality Monday when nine youngsters from the Model City Neighborhood left for 6 weeks of camping at Mayhew Island, Newfound Lake.

For most of the boys it will be their first camping experience. Jon Choate has planned a full program for the boys, including swimming boating camping, fishing and other activities designed to encourage self confidence and initiative.

Model City officials said that the projectis funded by the Pasquaney Trust and the Groton School Camp Association. It is hoped that next summer about 40 boys will take part in the program.

The boys, all of whom were selected by the Citizen's Policy Committee of the Model City Agency are: Paul Anderson, Emile Krajewski, Tom Luksza, Tom Szelog, Marty Paquette, Billy Baric, George Reiley, David Jutras, Robert Marchwicz.

Mayor John C. Morgan and other Model City Agency officials were on hand to see the boys off.

Chris Spirou, chairman of the Citizen's Policy Committee said that this program is significant because it represents the first real fruits of the past year's labor. We know that many people have been wondering if the Model City program has done any actual programming. Mayhew Island signals the beginning of many programs and projects designed to fulfill the many needs of the model neighborhood. It is only a first of a series of recreational services for both children and adults to be implemented during the next year.

gram in 1994.

But regardless of our history, traditions, and established policies, the success of the boys and program is fragile and only made real through hard work and commitment.

It is indeed a special privilege to be at the very heart of this remarkable program and to be able to touch each person on the island in a meaningful way. Donors and supporters make their mark and contribute to our growing and rich folklore and history of Mayhew. But most importantly, Mayhew leaves a lasting impression in the hearts and minds of the boys we serve.

THE MAYHEW MISSION

Mayhew is a preventive program that strives to encourage the positive social, emotional, physical, and behavioral development of at-risk New Hampshire boys, so that they can become happy, successful, and contributing members of their communities. Moreover, Mayhew strives to serve as a lifelong support community for these boys as they mature.

CANDIDATES

Candidates for the Mayhew Program are 10 and 11-year-old New Hampshire boys from low-income families. The vast majority live in single-parent households and participate in the program tuition-free. Referrals to the program can be made by school officials, youth counselors, clergy, social workers, families, and friends in February and March of each year.

The ideal candidate for Mayhew is a boy who will respond to the positive support of the Mayhew community; who will appreciate the opportunity to learn new skills and share in group experiences; who needs a boost of self-confidence; and who is eager to make a new start for himself. Before beginning his involvement with Mayhew, each boy must make a commitment to try his hardest, to try everything, and to try to get along with others.

THE ISLAND CHALLENGE

The Mayhew experience begins for each boy with the Island Challenge: a rigorous and challenging four-week summer camp experience on Mayhew Island. The summer program promotes the development of improved self-esteem and behavior, healthier peer interactions, goal settting skills, and a strong sense of belonging.

During the Island Challenge, boys spend one of two four-week residential sessions on Mayhew Island in Newfound Lake. There, in a highly structured group-oriented setting, each boy is encouraged to participate in challenging group and individual activities; he receives public praise and rewards for outstanding effort and improvement; and he is given the opportunity to establish for himself a new reputation in a fair and positive environment. Mayhew hopes that each boy learns that he alone is responsible for his actions, and that he has a clear choice throughout the day: either participate fully and peacefully, or be isolated from the group. Mayhew's structured setting, combined with frequent public praise and positive reinforcement, encourages increased self-worth, improved behavior, and high achievement.

Zach and Alex

Michelle Bowie

Shan Heslop & Jordan—ready to climb

ON THE ISLAND

The cabin group constitutes the core unit on the Island. All boys belong to a 7 member cabin group that goes by a unique name, like the Volunteers or Leviathan. Boys participate in all regular activities and meals as part of their cabin group. This provides ample opportunity to promote constructive group interactions. Discipline at Mayhew is clear, fair, and calm. If a boy acts inappropriately, he is isolated from the group and later given a choice to discuss the situation with his cabin counselor. If he is not respectful, or if a serious event like a fight breaks out, he is taken to the lodge to spend time with the lodgemaster. The lodgemaster will go through a similar cycle until the boy demonstrates that he is respectful and ready to talk. He will then be returned to his group with a clean slate and every opportunity to contribute to his cabin group.

ISLAND ACTIVITIES

WORK HOUR

At daily work hours, boys work together on a variety of projects and are paid in "Mayhew money," the island currency, according to how well they work. The importance of diligence, listening to and following instructions, and working as a team are emphasized. Boys get to spend their Mayhew money a couple of times a week at the Mayhew Market.

ATHLETICS

Group athletics on the island include softball, basketball, floor hockey, and soccer. The emphasis is placed on improvement, sportsmanship, and effort.

CREW ROWING

Rowing is practiced on the island in basic 7-man dories and demands that the boys learn to work together as a unit to be successful.

PROJECT ADVENTURE

Project Adventure is an experiential education program utilizing group initiatives as well as both low-rope and high-rope activities in order to promote group cohesiveness, group problem-solving, group cooperation, group trust, and an acceptance of challenge. Mayhew is home to an extensive challenge course including many unique and quite-challenging high element climbing events as well many low-element group obstacles and initiatives.

HIKING

Hiking involves ascending two mountain peaks in the White Mountain National Forest as a cabin group activity. The boys use this challenge to strengthen their role with their cabin group, to enjoy the natural splendors of the White Mountains, and to demonstrate their positive and supportive behavior outside the confines of the island. One of the highest end-

John & Jon

Alex

SWIMMING
Swim instruction is conducted daily as part of a Red Cross certified program. The hour-long period usually begins with some warmup drills, followed by intensive instruction. Boys that work hard and can be trusted to swim out to the raft by themselves may qualify to become a Raft Rat. There is also a Miler's club for boys who swim a mile over the course of the session.

ACHIEVEMENT PROGRAM
An individual achievement program is conducted four days a week in the late-afternoon. Boys choose an activity to pursue from a variety of areas, including watersports, art and crafts, chess, science, etc. and can earn a basic, intermediate, or advanced ribbon for demonstrated effort, knowledge and skill. Good performance in the achievement program, combined with good leadership and citizenship, earns an invitation to the Director's Outer Circle, the Island honor society. The ultimate honor is the Director's Inner Circle.

COOKOUTS
Every Wednesday and Saturday night we hold cookouts at individual cabin group sites around the island. The cookouts are a fine time to relax as a group and take a break from the regular structure of the program.

COMMUNITY NIGHTS
Community nights, held twice a week after cookouts, are an opportunity for boys and staff to spend time together, share talents, and talk about the values that bind us together. We sing songs, tell stories, perform skits, and generally enjoy each other's company.

ARTS PROGRAM
Started in 2004, Mayhew's Arts Program gives the boys a chance to express themselves creatively, while teaching them some basic techniques they can use at home. A focus on teamwork is still central, and the boys are encouraged to collaborate on several different group projects.

COMMUNITY OUTREACH
To continue to build on his progress and further develop a relationship with him, Mayhew's professional staff visits each boy at home and school throughout the year. During this Community Outreach phase of the program, the staff act as positive role models for the boys while encouraging them to continue to make good choices. It is during a boy's second full year in the program when he typically makes even greater progress and begins serving as a role model for the less experienced boys.

Gavin at bat.

John Lynch & Cameron

As the boys return home after the summer, Mayhew begins its community outreach phase. From September to May each year, Mayhew's five community workers visit regularly the boys in their respective caseloads. These visits with the boys serve to reinforce the lessons of the summer and build on Mayhew's relationship with each boy. Essentially, the staff are positive role models while advocating for the boys at home and at school. They provide a sympathetic and often tension-defusing ear to family conflicts, they provide extensive written reports on each boy's summer experience to parents, school officials, and other involved agencies, but most importantly, they continue to serve as friends and role models for the boys of the program.

LINK-UP
Link-Up is the next step. Each Link, as the boys are known, may participate for up to four more years. Thus, Links can maintain their connection to Mayhew through their teenage years. They continue to receive guidance, encouragement, and role modeling through visits at home by Mayhew's staff and during their week-long summer session at the Mayhew Base House. Link-Up strives to encourage community service, social and individual responsibility, and work experience.

The culmination of the Mayhew experience for many alumni is to return as staff members. This provides great depth in maintaining the Mayhew traditions and the role modeling essential to the program. Each alumni staff receives college scholarships funds matching his salary.

In response to a variety of surveys in the early 90's (and our perception that our graduates deserve a more active, official connection with Mayhew), we founded, in 1994, the Mayhew Link-Up program. Link-Up has proven to be both an effective way to stay in touch with Mayhew's grauduates and a way to create an image of success and community involvement, which the current Mayhew boys can aspire to achieve.

As Links, Mayhew boys continue to participate in the year-round, follow-up visits with full time staff members. During the summer, while the 10-12 year-old program boys are on the Island, Mayhew Links are taking on more and more responsibility out in the community. They come to the basehouse for a busy week that is mainly focused on planning, preparing, and executing a two to three day canoeing or hiking trip. Whether they're paddling down the Saco River or trekking through the White Mountains, Links are working with the staff to ensure the success of each expedition. Their efforts pay off year after year, and the Link-Up week has become an important part of the summer for many boys.

The Mayhew Achievers cabin group (2003)

Above "Links" includes L-R; Moises & Sabastion

KITCHEN STAFF: LINKS GIVING BACK

Another great opportunity is available to boys who have been through both their two years on the Island and completed one year of Link-Up. These "second year Links" can apply to work in the Island kitchen. Now behind the counter, the kitchen staff serve not just as cooks and dishwashers, but also as role models and examples of the importance of hard work and commitment. In exchange for all their efforts, kitchen staff earn real paychecks, which are matched dollar for dollar in a personal education fund.

SUPPORT FOR THE BOYS OF MAYHEW

Mayhew boys receive full scholarships to participate. Their cost is the commitment they must make and a meager $10 enrollment fee. To support them, we have a great deal of money to raise and are fortunate to have many loyal and generous donors. Support for Mayhew derives from seven NH United Ways; Merrimack County, Greater Manchester, Monadnock, Lakes Region, Greater Seacoast, Upper Valley, and North Country.

The other contributions are derived from an annual appeal to individuals, foundations, businesses, and service clubs. We do not have exclusive development staff and do not engage in fund raising activities outside of generating interest in the program from individuals and organizations. Our funding comes directly from people who know our mission and lend a hand through their financial support. We have a very active Board of Trustees, who participate 100% in our Annual Fund. Furthermore, the Mayhew Trustees show extraordinary leadership in our financial development. They completed the Capital Campaign for the Base House in 1998 and continuously help attract additional endowment funds for the future of our program.

The Mayhew Program is available to boys from New Hampshire. The number of boys from each community is based on the support we receive from that community. Most of our boys thus come from the seven United Way areas where we are a partner agency.

The "Ravens" cabin group (2007)

"The Assorted Candy" cabin group (2007)

THE REFERRAL PROCESS

Boys referred to Mayhew are ten or eleven years old and have experienced either some social difficulties or lack of opportunities. Each year we choose from over 200 candidates after extensive screening and interviewing. We accept referrals from principals, teachers, counselors, social workers, Boys and Girls Club directors, youth athletic program staff, probation officers, and other youth officials from many areas throughout New Hampshire from mid-February to mid-March each year.

The selection process is based on our attempt in determining which boys will benefit the most from the program. We weigh many objective factors including family income, family make-up, candidate age, and many subjective factors like apparent need and ability to benefit from the program. We then interview the best prospects, beginning in April, and make our final selections for the summer by May.

Invariably, the boys see Mayhew as a chance that may seem too good to be true. We try hard to undersell the program and emphasize at each step the serious commitment the boy and family must make. The boys come to Mayhew of their own will and are granted the chance to determine for themselves if this is something they can commit to. Once they commit themselves to participate, to work hard, and to abide by a high standard, this is really the beginning of Mayhew for them. Their departure from shore and journey to the Island only makes it tangible for them. They have really already begun.

All boys participate in the program tuition-free thanks to our many friends and supporters.

Mayhew is an independent non-profit agency also belonging to the New Hampshire United Ways of Greater Manchester, Greater Seacoast, Lakes Region, Merrimack County, Monadnock, North Country, and the Upper Valley.

2nd session 2005

"The Roots" cabin group. (2006)

"Da Rappin Kangaroos" cabin group. (2006)

Paul submerged

Matt Fifield—then & now.

{Year-Round Staff}

(Clockwise)

Jim Nute, Executive Director

Michelle Bowie, Director of Admin.

Ed Thompson, Program Director

Matt Simon, Community Outreach

Jon Eaton, Community Outreach

Ken Fuller, Community Outreach

Greg Stoutzenberger, Community Outreach

Matt Fifield, Community Outreach

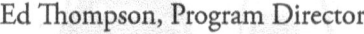

OFFICERS

Timothy A. Gudas, Concord, President
Alan M. Cantor, Concord, Vice-President
Michael J. Kennedy, Manchester, Treasurer
William D. Davies, Jr., Greenwich CT Secretary

TRUSTEES:
Susan (Sammy) Baldini
Thomas H. Berry
Richard H. Beyer
Sandy Colhoun
Richard T. Cowern
Roberta A. Daly
Jane A. Foster
Audrey S. Hagerman
David E. Howe

TRUSTEES:
Suzanne M. Lee
Paul J. McGoldrick
T. Holmes Moore
Thomas J. Obrey
John Richards II
Jeffrey Shackett
Nicholas Silitch
Dianne M. Walsh-Green
Todd Warden

TRUSTEE EMERITI:
Carl B. Jacobs, Sr.,
Robert M. Larson
Robert Rier

MORE MENTIONS AND PROFILES

Dave Bird	The philosophical center of the program, a man who remains a thoughtful and inspiring friend to many on the staff and perhaps the person most responsible for helping Mayhew become a program that prizes and encourages genuine, low-key and focused role modeling in the relationships between and among the staff and the boys.
Michelle Bowie	Where would Mayhew be without her?! 26 Years and counting of making Mayhew a smooth-running organization and a truly special place.
Al Cantor	A key figure in making Mayhew what it is today – a strong program for the boys and a model organization. Executive Director from 1984-1995, current trustee and mentor to so many of the staff and the Board.
Henry "Sam" Chauncey, Jr.	A former GSC staff member, a founding Mayhew trustee and a lifelong friend and guide to the program.
Jon Choate	Mayhew's first-ever Director and a lifelong friend of the program.
Tony Governanti	Responsible for nurturing Mayhew forward as a program from its nascent stages through to the mid-80's.
Dave Howe	From being a role model to the boys of Groton School Camp as a summer staff member to being one of Mayhew's finest role models and catalysts toward meaningful action as a trustee of the program decades later, Dave has simply never stopped making a huge difference!
Roger Larochelle	A very long history with Mayhew, which spanned the 70's to his own years as Executive Director 1995-2003.
Owen S. Lindsay	A founding trustee and role model for so many, truly a key figure in making Mayhew happen and in building its strength over many years.
Don Magaw	For more than 20 years, a Mayhew institution as Director of Maintenance and an inspiring father figure to many boys and staff.
Jim Nute	Jim considers himself to be the luckiest guy in the world to share in the love of his family and to be helping spread GSC's and Mayhew's reach to a whole new generation of tremendous boys.
Jack Richards	A former GSC staff member, a founding and current trustee – the longest serving member of the Board, and a fount of upbeat strength and leadership.
Mark "Doc Schie" Schiewetz	Longtime Mayhew staffer and the man who brought the high climbs and Project Adventure to Mayhew Island. Mark remains an excellent and close friend to the program.
Juanita Woodward	Cook and the take-no-nonsense heart of the Island kitchen for more than 15 years.

THE MAYHEW PROGRAM

TONY GOVERNANTI, 1971, showing the ropes. Tony's service; 1970-1984 (First Mayhew Executive Director)

AL CANTOR, 2006, from the re-dedication of "Cantor Yards"—the Mayhew ballfield. Al's Service: Summer Staff 1975 & 1976, Year-Round Staff 1982-1984, Executive Director 1984-1995, Trustee.

ROGER LAROCHELLE, 2002, welcoming Corey to the "Outer Circle" —the Island honor society. Roger's service: Summer Staff 1975-1978, Year-Round Staff 1979-1981, Executive Director 1995-2003.

JIM NUTE, 2006, welcoming Josh to the Outer Circle. Jim's service: Summer Staff 1990 &1991, Year-Round Staff 1991-2001, Executive Director 2003-Present.

The Mayhew Program is 35 percent of the history—in total years—but given only eight percent of this book's pages. I'm sure someday a grateful Mayhew Alum will do Volume II. KB

For copies of this book,
Contact The Mayhew Program

The Mayhew Program
P.O. Box 120
Bristol, NH 03222
(603) 744-6131
http://www.mayhew.org/
mayhew@mayhew.org

....

Or, order on-line from:
Grotonschoolcamp.com

All Proceeds From This Book Go To The
The Mayhew Program

THE MAYHEW PROGRAM, a direct descendant of the Groton School Camp, is a preventive program that strives to encourage the positive, social, emotional, physical, and behavioral development of at-risk New Hampshire boys, so that they can become happy, successful, and contributing members of their communities. Moreover, Mayhew strives to serve as a lifelong support community for these boys as they mature.

Courtesy of Bill Hemmel, Lakes Region Aerial Photo

THE EDITOR, KEN BINGHAM, was born the youngest of seven in 1947 in Brockton, Massachusetts. His father died in 1955 leaving his mother to raise the rambunctious four boys and three girls alone. Toughing it out, she raised all of them successfully.

Bingham has especially fond memories of his camping days at Groton School Camp. Mr. Paul Abry was the Camp director then. According to Bingham, "Mr. Abry and the Groton School Staff ran a wonderful program for us ragamuffins, and treated us special. Summer Camp was a big deal for us kids."

Bingham's passion lately is to help nonprofits—like Mayhew—promote their organization through the use of their own rich history.

The Mayhew Program
1969-Present

PO Box 120

Bristol, NH 03222

603) 744-6131

mayhew@mayhew.org

http://www.mayhew.org

www.ingramcontent.com/pod-product-compliance
Lightning Source LLC
Chambersburg PA
CBHW080332170426
43194CB00014B/2536